THE
POWER
GAME

THE POWER GAME

HOW TO USE THE BLACK ART OF
CORPORATE AND PERSONAL POWER
TO GET THE RESULTS YOU WANT

GERRY **GRIFFIN**

CAPSTONE

First published 1999 by
Capstone US
Business Books Network
163 Central Avenue
Suite 2
Hopkins Professional Building
Dover
NH 03820
USA

Capstone Publishing Limited
Oxford Centre for Innovation
Mill Street
Oxford OX2 0JX
United Kingdom
http://www.capstone.co.uk

CIP catalogue records for this book are available from the British Library and the US Library of Congress

ISBN 1-900961-99-7

Typeset in 10/14 pt Century Schoolbook by
Sparks Computer Solutions Ltd, Oxford
http://www.sparks.co.uk
Printed and bound by
T.J. International Ltd, Padstow, Cornwall

This book is printed on acid-free paper

Substantial discounts on bulk quantities of Capstone books are available to corporations, professional associations and other organizations. If you are in the USA or Canada, phone the LPC Group for details on (1-800-626-4330) or fax (1-800-243-0138). Everywhere else, phone Capstone Publishing on (+44-1865-798623) or fax (+44-1865-240941).

For Bronagh

"The Protector has always said that a populace which in general assents to its ruling – and to its rulers – needs few sheriffs and no troops"

Iain M. Banks, *Inversions*

Contents

Foreword

Of all the factors that influence individual behaviour and collective action in social settings, power is perhaps the most difficult to come to grips with. The problem is that power has the characteristic of an all or nothing variable. Without any doubt, it is a very important factor. In this book Gerry Griffin uses the analogy of electricity, and he is right. Like electricity, it is not immediately visible. And, like electricity, most things will not work without it. But, once you wear the spectacles that make power visible, then everything is seen as power-related. Every phenomenon, every action, every constraint, every passion – all become causes or consequences of a power game. As a result, observers and analysts of social behaviour tend to fall in one of two categories – those who see the world through the lens of power, and see everything as manifestations of power, and those who do not and, therefore, do not see power at all. A majority, myself included, fall in the second category. This is perhaps why, as Gerry identifies in this book, 'power is America's last dirty word.' 'Not just America's,' is all I will add to that comment.

There is a form of power – coercive power – that can be clearly separated from other kinds of attitudes and feelings like those of love, trust and respect, and other kinds of motivations such as ideology, vision and even altruism. The prison guard exercises coercive power. This form of power is simple to understand and analyse and that is also why this form of power is not very interesting. All other forms of power – particularly, normative power – have a complex mix of causes and consequences. It is precisely this mix that makes the separation of the power dimension from the others so difficult and is also why it is these forms of power that are much more interesting to understand and analyse.

And this is where the value of this book lies. This book views the world through a lens that makes power visible and, therefore, can provide a power-related interpretation of phenomena as diverse as teleworking, the Internet, leadership and environmental activism.

I do not believe that the interpretations Gerry provides are complete. Alternative analysis can be provided, to complement his interpretations. But, that does not deny the value of the lens through which the readers can see the world. Power happens, and it is useful to recognise how it happens. *The Power Game* is simple, perhaps too simple – but that is also the strength of the book. It will sensitize readers to one aspect of most day-to-day phenomena that the scores of other books on organization, management or leadership tend to ignore. It will give them an additional lens, to complement the others they already have. As a result, they will have the ability to enrich the variety of perspectives through which they can see the world.

Finally, I also know Gerry to be a liberal who has an intrinsic dislike for either being subject to someone else exercising power over him, or in overtly or even covertly exercising power over anyone else. He has observed that executives often like to have power, for the sake of having power, and deep-down, he does not like that very much. He has also seen that the rhetoric of empowerment is often just that, a rhetoric, and simply a different way of exercising power. That too offends his liberal values. So, the book really is his contribution to help people see the power game, so as to break free from it. Yes, having written it he will like as many people being exposed to it as possible, but that is not why he has written the book. He has written it because he would like the world to be a better place – with less tyranny, less prisoners of power, more self-actualization and more personal liberty.

Sumantra Ghoshal

Preface

The first question when entering on a project as daunting and time consuming as a book is why? The concept of power is something that has long fascinated me partly because it is in some ways a "secret garden": the ways of power are mostly concealed but every so often one can catch a glimpse of something fascinating over the wall, some aspect of power in action.

And there is a draw. We are automatically drawn towards people of power not just because of what power they might have over us, but also to witness the exercise of power itself: to watch them wield power over others. From Gandhi to Gates, we witness the wide range of principles that are invoked to make this power exercise possible: one the freedom of his nation, the other freedom of consumer choice.

But this fascination is not just to do with these worthy principles. It is prompted by the activity of power itself. Power is also a paradox because it not only draws us in, but its excess and corrupting influences also repel us. In writing an extended essay on power like this, one feels the need to put some distance between oneself and the subject. As has been remarked, "power is America's last dirty word." And the world of business is one of the few terrains left where one can exercise extreme forms of power over another without any public censure. In attempting a simple non-scientific excursion into the use of corporate power, I feel a sense of trepidation.

My initial desire was to look at the logical use of power in the pursuit of owner value, a central if not sole aim of organized business. But to be that logical; to mobilize one's staff and resources rigorously in the pursuit of owner value itself is a dangerous occupation because there is always an element of exploitation involved. Ultimately in business, your employees produce your corporate value but usually do not share many of the spoils.

Will it always be so? Employees have not been and probably will not be replaced by robots.

In fact there is more discussion these days in business schools about intellectual capital (the corporate assets that are within the workforce) than ever before. Much management training is devoted to ways in which that intellectual capital can be unlocked and released in the pursuit of further value.

In is also a fact that, as we close off on this millennium, the vast majority of corporations have still to find ways of properly releasing that intellectual capital. Most are still locked into command, control and compliance economies. Within these traditional systems, we find the exercise of power central to most endeavors. Power in these corporations is still often an end in itself. It is this "aphrodisiac" quality of power, its seductive and dangerous draw which lies behind the veil of many an executive decision. If the decisions are taken in the name of competitive advantage, they are praised. If they are to further an individual advantage, they are seen as merely political. Quite often it is impossible to tell the difference.

Before embarking on the research for this book, I spoke with an esteemed professor of organizational behavior. He told me: "We don't teach power at the School because it is too hard. We could offer some Foucault, but what is an MBA student going to make of Foucault?" He continued: "We tell them (i.e. the MBAs) to read Machiavelli's *The Prince* – and we leave it at that."

In many ways, *The Prince* is an excellent introduction to the world of naked power. In a series of warfaring cameos, Machiavelli extrapolates a number of "rules of thumb" for increasing the effectiveness of one's power base. Machiavelli is also an apt reference point for *The Power Game* because *The Prince* is, in my view, a very practical excursion. Machiavelli does not tell the reader that he *should* engage in the type of activities he describes. Rather, *if* one wants to get ahead in the scenarios he discusses, then what he offers are useful practical insights. In this way, Machiavelli is not the ultimate in evil as some have contended, but the ultimate pragmatist.

The Power Game also attempts a pragmatic, rather than ethically riven, appraisal to the use of power in a corporate setting. In fact, I have invited Niccolo Machiavelli himself to "guest" in the book and engage in a discussion about each game scenario with an aspiring executive who wants to increase his own power base.

Never has there been a time in which the corporation has felt itself under such a siege. Never has there been a more apt time to explore the dark art of the exercise of power...

Enjoy the game.

Acknowledgments

Special thanks to the faculty, staff and students of London Business School. In particular, Professors Paul Willman, John Hunt, Paddy Barwise, Sumantra Ghoshal and Don Sull.

To the top PR team – Pippa, Sandra, Mika and Richard. Fergus Lynch, Mary Hardie. The whole Griffin and Begley clans, Michael Paul-Gallagher, Dr Ciaran Parker, Professor Tom Docherty, Martin Langford, Paul Gillions, Perry Yeatman, Per Heggenes, Nick Bent, and the dynamic trio: Rebecca, Rachel and Andrea. To the gurus of Suntop Media – Stuart and Des. Tim "Quicksilver" Izli. Zoe and Patsy.

Special thanks to Jim Griffin (Essential Media); and Vicky Carnes, Mike Austin and Pete Austin of mbagames.com in the development of thepowergame.com

How to Play the Game

The games in this book are based on a simple methodology, which is explained in detail. Once you have got the hang of the methodology, the game can be used to address a wide variety of business issues. The methodology forms the basis of a training workshop and senior executives from several billion-dollar corporations have already been "playing the game" in order to rethink their strategies on a range of issues – from dealing with activists through to rethinking the issue of pricing transparency in different markets.

As with all games, you first need to familiarize yourself with the rules and then practice some games for yourself. The book, in a sense, is written to help you prepare to play games, specific to your own personal/corporate situation.

The airplane game (p. 9) is an excellent example of a game that is quickly accessible. Flying on an aircraft is a common experience in being the object in an extreme example of power-relations. You can readily see the maneuvers and ruses employed by the carrier to make customers compliant and to allow them to run the service in an economically viable way. For it is the latter that is the real pay-off of such power relations: running an air service and maintaining a high degree of control over the passengers has more to do with making a profit than with passenger safety.

There are two levels of game detailed in this book: *personal* and *corporate* power games. Personal power games are concerned with how an individual can assess how an organization can exercise control over him. In the Call-Center and the Teleworking games you will see *how* an organization can exercise control over you. The third game on the personal level – the Technology game – shows how the individual can begin to subvert the power relation over him and get some power for himself. This is not merely an academic pursuit – we are all locked into unproductive power relations and need to get out of them in order to get more money or promotion.

This is precisely how the first section ends – with some games that you need to fill out (with help!), which will prepare you for negotiating your pay-rise and promotion.

Once you have addressed the issue of personal power, you then need to see how you can exercise it on behalf of the organization: *corporate* power games. These are games that will help you combat external forces threatening the power base of your organization – activists, competitors and so forth. Again, having identified how to play the power game at a corporate level, you can then go on to play some games of your own. There are some examples with which you can start, such as the Market Dominance game, which shows you how to fend off attack by a competitor on your market share.

Here are some tips on using the book to best advantage:

- Gain an understanding of how power works (see the *Power Donut*) and how belief and fear are two fundamental tools to create and maintain advantageous power relations.
- Gain an understanding of the methodology in action (e.g. the airplane game) so that you can use the methodology for games that are relevant to you in your position and relevant to your corporation.
- Use the "prompt questions" to identify the relevance of each game for you.
- Read the sections dealing with *Power Games and the Individual.* Then try out the games on that level – they deal with getting a pay-rise and promotions. If you are in the enviable position of needing no further promotions or money, do try the games for yourself anyway – the practice will be important for level two when you will look at exercising power on behalf of the corporation.
- Use the blank templates at the back of the book, which will guide you to frame games specific to your business.
- See the Appendix, which contains an explanation of how each element of the game methodology should work.

- Go to www.thepowergame.com should you need any help with a game or with framing a game of your own.

INTRODUCTION

What is Power?

Power is fear

Something was about to happen. We were in the penthouse boardroom. The eyes of my colleague were darting over my shoulder, squinting nervously at the horizon. I looked in the same distant direction. A large speck appeared and grew larger. A fearful shudder Mexican-waved around the cedarwood table. A name was silently mouthed, like some Yahweh whose name was forbidden to be publicly pronounced. The CEO was on his way, the drone of the helicopter his only warning.

The nervous shivering of the top executives fell into sync with the heavy chugging sound of the helicopter as the CEO alighted on the roof. He was feet above our heads. The room fell silent. We believed we could hear his footsteps.

In that boardroom I witnessed power at work. I felt it. What was clear to me was that fear ruled this organization. Not just fear of losing one's job – of being fired. The firing policy seemed so indiscriminate and arbitrary that it would have been no real disgrace to have been sent packing. No, the fear was undefined yet palpable. Perhaps it was a fear unique to each individual. Maybe the CEO and the cult of that CEO were merely a canvas upon which each aspiring executive painted his/her own career insecurities and terrors. Maybe the CEO was really a nice guy. But as he strode out of the helicopter he did look unbalanced to me.

Power is faith

In the 1980s, Big Jim Brown[1] was hailed as a corporate messiah. The football-playing ex-captain of the Cleveland Browns had achieved major productivity gains at RMI, a subsidiary of US Steel. Big Jim's campaign was spearheaded by the "smile" as both logo and rhetorical device. Niles, Ohio (where they were based) was replaced by "Smiles," Ohio.

Big Jim also encouraged sayings such as "if you see a man without a smile, give him one of yours." Productivity went up 80 per cent, union grievances down from 300 to 20.

The people had faith in Big Jim. They believed in Big Jim, as an icon, as a friend to the worker, as a football hero. Faith brought about a leap in productivity. They believed in Big Jim (the rhetoric) although they served the "real interests" of productivity. Faith was the foundation of Big Jim's power.

Power is a game

When researching this book, I had many conversations with learned professors who have spent decades teaching, directing, scrambling and unscrambling top executives from around the world. Some have kept detailed notes on what drives these executives to succeed. In the view of many of these academics, the men and women who attend their executive programs are mostly driven by the quest for power.

The data also suggest that women are as driven by this quest as their male colleagues.

The academics are not talking about power in order to achieve other things – to bring about a realization of personal ideas, aspirations and visions. No, it was power as an end in itself acting like a drug that attracts and binds the aspiring executives into savoring its pleasures. Put like this, power becomes a game, in the sense that it generates its own set of rules and can be enjoyed on its own – "neat," as it were, without need for further justification.

According to the Stanford's Jeffrey Pfeffer, organizational politics and power are closely identified:

> *"The concepts of power and organizational politics are related; most authors, myself included, define organizational politics as the exercise or use of power ..."*[2]

An article in the *Financial Times* by London Business School Professor John Hunt discusses the fact that anxieties about corporate politics

> *"... are most often expressed by people in their 30s as they begin to realise that their career is not a dress rehearsal; that peers with better political skills may pass them by ... It is a time when the importance of politics and patronage in medium to large organisations becomes undeniable."*

We will come to a more formal definition of the game soon. Suffice to say, a game involves a ruse – when there is more going on than meets the eye. It is this that upsets the "people in their 30s" that John Hunt refers to.

Power is all

We see it everywhere. It seems to involve people either believing in something, being inspired by words or deeds, and then willingly submitting to the will of the other; or indeed, as with the helicopter, it involves some abstract fear that perhaps expresses itself as a separate and individual fear for everyone. Power is fear. Power is faith (or belief). Power is a game.

We are all confronted by the quest for power at some stages in our careers. At some point we all want power, because power is invariably a measure of our success as well as the means to further that success. But to get ahead in your own personal track to success, to be that figure in the distance "getting on planes," how do you master the art of power; the dark art of the practice of power?

Do you have to wait your turn as in many Asian firms – waiting for age and experience, like some escalator upon which one passively waits for ascent having selected the step? Is there no way in which you can clamber up the steps past the "deadbeats"? Yes you can put in the hours; kiss the right butts; be a member of the right clubs; apply your skills in the best possible way. But will that be enough? It seems so easy for others as they glide into the right areas. What do you need to do?

To understand and answer these questions one must first understand how power is used and how it is used efficiently. The power relations that exist on board an airplane are a good example. Perhaps you are on an aircraft as you read this.

The airplane as an example of the efficient and commercial use of power

◆ Do you ever feel powerless on a plane?
◆ Do you feel you the need to ask permission for very basic things, e.g. using the lavatory?
◆ Have you ever wondered why the pilots wear military-style uniforms?
◆ Do you feel greater "power" when in possession of a higher status ticket, e.g. business or first?

Think about it: you have precious little power, and this is not just based on your technical inability to fly a plane. First off, you are allocated a specific space (seat). In fact the organization of space on the craft would seem to be key to making power operate generally.

When do you sit down? When you are permitted. When can you stand up? When you are permitted. When can you smoke or take off your seat belt? Again, when you are permitted. This is not just in the name of safety in whose name, of course, such power relations are wielded.

Let us go further. What type of food can you eat? What seat can you sit in? These are determined by the contract into which you have entered with the carrier, but the organization of seating *is the way in which* the power relations determined by the contract are actually expressed. This is an important point. The allocation of seating not only reflects the contract with the carrier; it is also the way in which the carrier leverages power over you once you are on board. You have more control over the stewards when you book first than when you book coach. True?

Let us go further still. When can you sleep? Anytime, but on long-haul flights the carriers often run warm air through the cabins to make you drowsy (giving the stewards a rest) and run fresher air through the cabins (for example on the overnights) when they wish to serve breakfast.

Being on an airplane is a true experience in entering into quite an extreme form of power relations. The issue of safety, which would on the face of it warrant many of the personal restrictions you encounter, is in fact only responsible for some. There are other economic and operational reasons why you get treated the way you do. For example, to allow the stewards to serve all the passengers adequately and the carrier to put the minimum number of staff on each flight.

This is not a criticism of the flying experience. In fact, these power relations are necessary for the complete and commercially successful functioning of the carrier.

What is also interesting is that these extreme forms of power are exercised over us without any coercion, and without any show of superior strength. You see those pretty ornamental ropes sectioning off the different flight classes: first, business and coach? These ropes do perform a simple function in demarcating the various zones. These also act as symbols (this time economic) of what is and what is not permitted to you the traveller.

Ask yourself the question: are you on the inside or the outside of the braided cord? Is it permitted for you to step outside but not step inside? That is to ask, as a business traveller, whether you can go down into coach (without permission) to have a conversation with a friend. In coach, can you enter into business (without licence) and have a conversation with a friend in business? You see, the space begins to take on varying values and this indicates how the space on board is being used to leverage power over you.

While talking symbols, let us also remark on the military-type uniforms of the "captains." Again, of course they are not really military personnel, but the uniform acts as a symbol (this time safety) of the power invested in him by the airline with whom you have entered into a contract.

The airline does not actually have to exert any real coercion in order to gain and maintain considerable control over you. You conform and do what is required, partly through experience and knowledge of what is required. You do what is required by acknowledging a series of signs and symbols throughout the craft, most but not all of which are in the name of safety. But most fundamentally, the organization of space on the craft – that itself is the profound means that makes this whole exercise possible.

A humorous end-point by way of illustration: in mid-1998 a captain working with Go!, the low-cost British Airways spin-off, held his passengers on board after landing for an hour until the person who had been smoking in the toilets owned up to the "crime." In fact the captain himself was arrested for "false imprisonment."

Let us systemize the airplane game so that we can apply the principles in other situations. We can do so using the following methodology. There is a more detailed explanation of each aspect of the methodology in Appendix I.

Thesis
What does the game seem to be about? (Usually revolves around a shared "value" such as "safety" or "freedom of choice.")

Roles
What is the role of each player?

Aim
What is the overall purpose of the game?

Power-principle
Which is the dominant principle: belief or fear?

Pay-off
What are the ulterior motives?

The airplane game

Thesis

Safety.

Roles

1 The passenger – the object in the power play.
2 The steward – the agent of power "looking after you" but also ensuring you comply with the on-board laws.
3 The captain – the ultimate source of power on-board; the absent authority – a disembodied voice: calm, benevolent and omnipotent.

Aim

Ensure total passenger compliance

Power-principle (more detail on this later)

Fear – being 30,000 feet in the air usually provides enough fear "raw material" for the carrier to work with and to ensure your compliance.

Pay-off

Smooth and commercially viable running of the service. For example: have you ever said to the steward "Actually I'm not hungry at the moment – could you get back to me in an hour?" It would just not be viable for the carrier to provide such individual service. The fact that you never question when you can eat is itself a tacit acknowledgement by you of the power the carrier has over you.

Before we embark on some games, let us pull together some of the principles we have already encountered anecdotally.

How Power Really Works: Introducing the Power Donut

Because power is a difficult and abstract concept, why don't we think of it as a building? I will call it the *power donut*. Understanding how this building works, will help you understand how power actually works in practice.

The building (see Fig. 1) is composed of two parts. One is a donut-shaped building in which you place those over whom you want to exercise power, e.g. employees. In the center we have a tower with a light which shines out towards the donut. You (the supervisor) sit in the room behind the light.

The donut is divided into individual cells in which each employee is placed. Each is separated from the other but the light from the tower shines right through the cell. This architecture sets up a specific information flow, which creates and then maintains the power relations between the supervisor and the employee.

The information flow in the power donut

The light picks out the employee and each and every action he engages in can be noted by the supervisor. In other words, the employee offers up near total information about himself and makes himself the object in the power relationship.

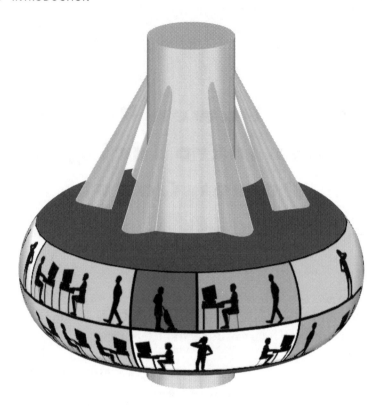

Fig. 1   A representation of the power donut.[3]

The second aspect of the information flow concerns what the employee might or might not know. Firstly, because he is separated from his other employees, he cannot find out any information "on the grapevine."

The donut separates or *individualizes* him. In fact, all the employee knows is that there is this constant light shining at him and that there *might* be somebody behind it looking at him. He is not certain of that. So while the supervisor knows all about the employee, the only thing that the employee knows is that the supervisor has the means (i.e. the light) to know everything. But he is not sure *when* he is being looked at. This system (i.e. an imbalance in the flow of information – the supervisor has more information than the employee) creates the conditions for a basic power relation.

But the power donut shows you how to not only create but also maximize power relations over another.

Maximizing power relations

The information accessible by the employee is uncertain. (Is the supervisor there? Is he not?) What is certain is that he might be! This paradox leads to the power relationship going up a step. Because the employee is not totally sure whether he is being watched at a particular moment, he will effectively end up governing himself. Because of the possibility of being supervised, we end up with the fact that he has to presume he is being watched at any time (regardless of whether there is anybody actually there or not).

What we see here amounts to an internalization of the power relations, i.e. the relationship has moved inside the inmate's own mind. Internalized power relations are the most time and resource efficient. The person being governed is doing most of the work to keep the power relationship in place.

The two principles of power: belief and fear

There are two principles (let's call them Power-Principles) in operation here.

- *Power-principle #1: belief.* This is the belief that the employee is being supervised – belief not just in the sense that the employee *believes* that he is being supervised. It goes deeper. We shall see in the discussion coming up that it is a *belief in the authority* of the supervisor; a belief in the system that places both employee and supervisor in that system (e.g. your employment) in the first place.
- *Power-principle #2: fear.* The second principle, that of fear, is more straightforward. It is fear of the possible coercive measures (psychological, economic or physical) that will be visited on the employee should he step out of line. The starting point in this equation is the

strategic or planned use of space into which the employee is placed. Remember the aircraft and how the seating plan was used to maintain power over you? The end point is a continuous and efficient power relationship over the employee.

Throughout *The Power Game* we will use the principles explored above. So let us sum up what the power donut teaches us about producing, maintaining and maximizing power relations:

- *Step 1*. Organize the space for the employee so that it produces a two-way and unbalanced information flow. This entails separating the employee from others and establishing a direct link between the employee and the center (the tower).
- *Step 2*. The unbalanced information flow means that you know everything about the employee, while all he or she knows is that you know everything.
- *Step 3*. This type of information flow will generate two states of mind – belief and fear – and sets up a basic power relationship.
- *Step 4*. These states of mind will create the conditions whereby the employee begins to govern himself. This is more resource efficient than constant supervision.

How Henry Ford used the power donut

Henry Ford's production line was a crude but effective use of the power donut. It needs to be pointed out, however, that the donut system can be applied more subtly; examples of this will be explored in the game.

Integral to Ford's success was the ability to produce a car at low cost to fulfil his vision of marketing a car which "will be so low in price that no man making a good salary will be unable to own one." Firstly, the car was produced in a strategic or planned space – the production line (step 1 above).

Step 1: separating the employees

"Ford believed in people getting on with their jobs and not raising their heads above functional parapets. He didn't want engineers talking to salespeople ..."[4]

Step 2: total knowledge

Ford's knowledge of the process was complete. He calculated that the production of the Model T required 7882 different operations among which "949 require strong, able bodies and practically physically perfect men. 3338 ordinary physical strength." The remainder, Ford calculated, "could be undertaken by women or older children." He adds, "we found 670 could be filled by legless men, 2637 by one-legged men, two by armless men, 715 by one-armed men and 10 by blind men."[5]

Step 3: a blend of belief and fear

Ford led with his passionate vision of the Model T and its place in society (corporate mission). He paid double the average industry wage (personal mission). Both of these inspired a belief or faith in his workforce. He also operated a ruthless environment in which Ford executives were widely spied on in case they began to make decisions for themselves (fear). Ford is also reputed to have physically kicked to pieces a version of the Model T which did not meet his approval (fear).

Step 4: self-governing

The Ford culture did not permit of any managers apart from Ford himself. Clearly the culture for the whole organization was to do his bidding as directly and as transparently as possible *as if he were actually present* at each moment. In other words, the work force would govern itself in a manner of which Ford would approve.

An imagined discussion between an aspiring executive and Machiavelli[6]

On board and strapped in I began to think about my career goals. How much I wanted to be earning in five years time? Easy. How much budget I wanted under my control? No problem. How many people under my control? Ballpark.

Let's get more specific. Let's discuss the veneer of the desk. Black with leather inlaid trimming? Nice. Small anteroom for some power naps in the afternoon, like Paul Newman in Towering Inferno. *Cool. Where are you going to be in five years time?*

Before my reverie could get a fix onto my red sports car, a slightly odd looking individual seated beside me looked up from his book, eager to chat. His large child-like eyes had a friendly tone. The overall effect though, undoubtedly aided by his black attire, was one of sombreness. Here was a man who reflected deeply upon profound matters.

"Niccolo" he said, his accent was more pronounced than I had first imagined.

"John" I replied with resignation. I didn't like company on company business. "On business?"

"Perhaps" he replied evenly.

We small-talked about the problems we had getting boarded for a while and then the conversation steered to what I had been scribbling on my note-pad.

"It's just my five-year career plan," I offered; "where I want to be, who I want to be, how much I want to be. You know, the usual aspirational executive kind of stuff."

I found him surprisingly easy to relate to, and I talked through all the problems at work. Getting sidelined. Getting under-noticed, under-rewarded, overworked.

"And why do you think it is thus?" he asked, as the steward brought us another round.

"I just can't seem to, you know." I struggled. "I feel ... impotent. I just can't seem to make it happen. Do you know what I mean?"

He looked like he did, although his confidence also told me that his knowledge wasn't based on experience of personal failure.

I continued: "To be successful at my career, in my business you need to have control, to exercise control. To have power ..."

"You are interested in power?" he asked, cutting across my self-indulgent musings.

"Yes," I said. "I suppose I am."

"Control is an expression of power," he continued, "but not what it is."

I looked slightly sceptical. His eyebrows arched in his high forehead. "Believe me, I have considered the subject for a very long time. You want to know how power works? How it can work for you?"

I nodded more enthusiastically.

"Well, I must caution you that power is a very difficult concept to grasp. And then, to exercise it and to do it well, that is more difficult again. Sometimes I think of power and its exercise in terms of your electrical power: you cannot really see it or touch it but without it things will not really work. Electrical power, while being very beneficial to humankind, is also capable of great destruction. Essentially it is a neutral force that we conceive in terms of its effects.

"In the same way, I think that power is neither good or bad. It can be utilized for what some might believe to be good as well as evil ends. Additionally, as I said, I think it easier to conceive of power in terms of its usage so that we can look at its impact. We do not want to get fixated on whether power relations change depending on context. That is too involved for here," he added gesturing deprecatingly around the plane. Let us keep the discussion of power as pertinent to a commercial context."

He continued. "The theory behind the power donut and the way it illustrates power is not just relevant to extreme totalitarian forms of power such as the prison or even the hospital. As we saw, it applies to more mundane everyday experiences such as on the car assembly line and even this aircraft.

"The theory holds for many different types of space – particularly the factory production line. Do not forget your Henry Ford's absolute control on the factory floor."

"Ford the control freak – who wanted to document every last thing involved in your job in order to control it?" I interjected.

"To an extent, yes," replied Niccolo.

Belief and fear as power-tools

We had just taken delivery of another round of drinks. Niccolo peered at his wine, holding it up to the light with interest.

"Something floating in it?" I asked.

"No, on the contrary, I was just admiring its clarity."

I began: "before you start on about your power donut, can I just tell you that all of this light and inmate stuff might work well hundreds of years ago. But today either fear reigns in the boardroom, or somehow the big cheese manages to inspire the workforce into doing his bidding."

"Out of love?" asked Niccolo.

I laughed. "No, let's call it belief – belief if you like in the whole being greater than the sum of the parts."

"And the great leader," added Niccolo, "perhaps manages to use both terror and love depending on what the situation merits?"

"You see," he continued, "the donut device will deliver both of these principles in a most satisfactory fashion – if used correctly.

"You must understand, though, exactly what is going on in the power donut in order to learn and then replicate. The first aspect of its operation involves the flow of information from the employee to the supervisor. The second involves the reverse in direction: if the information from the employee to the supervisor is the basis for knowledge, there is a second, even more profound transformation taking place within the inmate himself."

"And that is?"

"When the employees get installed in the power donut, they end up governing themselves because of either of two possibilities: firstly the belief that the supervisor is watching. Again, the apparatus was constructed so as to install a limited two-way information flow; all that was permitted to the inmate was unverifiable information about the

possible existence of the supervisor. This belief can also be extended further: perhaps a belief in the power system that placed the inmate in the apparatus in the first place? This might seem a little peculiar, but the fact remains that power needs to be legitimized and there is often a formal conferring process involved, which empowers the supervisor. We see this conferring process in action when a prime minster or president is sworn in; or when a priest/rabbi is decreed. Even when you receive a degree from a university (the degree being a symbol of elevated power), there is a formal conferring process.

Perhaps we can go further still in contending that belief has some positive value. Belief implies belief in something; perhaps even something worth believing in – the corporate mission? And this worth is something to which we can give a value. So when we talk about belief in the power sense (as inscribed by the power donut) we are talking more than just belief that the subject thinks that there could be a supervisor present. We are also talking about a belief in the system that placed him in that situation in the first place, for example the state and its impact on him."

I replied, "So what you are saying is that we are not just talking about believing that the boss could be lurking around the corner – but in fact a belief in the system like the 'corporation,' which has placed both you and that boss in that system in the first place."

"Precisely," said Niccolo. "And fear can work the same way – and in many respects act like the mirror image of belief. It can be privation of comforts; it can be physical or mental punishment; it can be loss of privilege – manifest or tacit – and so forth.

"But remember," added Niccolo, "what lies behind the ability to play on the beliefs and fears – indeed to create those beliefs and fears in each subject, lies in the way you organize the space around them."

"So Niccolo," I asked, "there are examples of power in action all around us. If I want to be powerful, I have to be able to learn how to instil beliefs or fears favorable to my cause?"

"Correct – but first you must understand how the organization can use space to lock you into a power relationship.

Our first set of games are personal power games: they concern how the individual is involved in a power relationship with his organization. The call-center game and the teleworking game will demonstrate how the organization can generate and maintain power over you. The third game, the technology game, will show you how the individual can subvert the corporate grip and begin to set up separate power bases.

We will then be able to play some corporate power games: games that concern the power relationships between the corporation and internal or external forces such as the media.

Notes

1   T. Peters & R. Waterman, *In Search of Excellence* (New York: Harper & Row, 1982).

2   J. Pfeffer, *Managing with Power* (Boston: Harvard Business School Press, 1994).

3   M. Foucault, *Discipline and Punish, The Birth of the Prison* (London: Penguin, 1991).

4   S. Crainer, *The Ultimate Book of Business Gurus* (Oxford: Capstone, 1998).

5   *Ibid.*

6   N. Machiavelli, *The Prince* (London: Penguin, 1995).

POWER GAMES AND THE INDIVIDUAL

Making Power

THE CALL-CENTER GAME

Each round of the game is divided into three segments:

1   The scene, in which the issues surrounding the particular power struggle are explored in a range of ways – analysis, examples and anecdotes.
2   The game itself, in which the various maneuvers are broken down and explored.
3   The discussion, in which the imaginary discussion between the aspiring executive and Niccolo Machiavelli continues.

The scene

In this first round of the game, we address the use of power over company employees in order to maximize productivity. In the last chapter, we saw how, in theory, the organization of space is key. To explore this at a practical level, we will take two modern work examples that show how space is used to manage the power relations with the employees. One is the modern phenomenon of teleworking – working from home – in which the worker is apparently able to rid himself of the dehumanizing effects of the workplace.

But to begin with, at the opposite end of the spectrum, there is the worker in the modern call-center. Call-centers are set up either to sell products over the telephone such as insurance, or to grow relations with the existing customer base (e.g. carelines).

The call-center: a return to Taylor's scientific management?

In 1911, the influential management-thinker Fredrick Taylor wrote:

> *"The work of every workman is fully planned out by the management at least one day in advance, and each man receives in most cases complete written instructions, describing in detail the task which he is to accomplish, as well as the means to be used in doing the work ... This task specifies not only what is to be done but how it is to be done and the exact time allowed for doing it."*[1]

The information about the work (the technical requirements, the technical competencies, the time allocated, the ability to measure precise output) means that the balance of power lies with the management. The management has an advantage because the work has been planned out in advance. All eventualities have already been foreseen by the management and each employee has been allocated a slot within the system.

It is clear that under this organization, the worker is the object of an advanced form of power relationship. But why? And how?

Direct Line Insurance: call-center pioneers

Direct Line Insurance (DLI) caused a revolution in the UK insurance business. Essentially, it did away with brokers and face-to-face contact and replaced it with a telemarketing operation backed up by comprehensive advertising and competitive pricing.

Founded in 1985, by 1997 it claimed over two million customers for its home insurance business and over eight hundred thousand customers for its home policy products.

In revolutionizing the financial services industry, DLI achieved and maintained a market leadership position in its field, despite severe price competition in the mid-1990s.

DLI currently handles 12 million calls per annum using just one thousand operators. It does this by tightly inter-relating technology, the telephone and the people,

To succeed in not only taking a leadership position in your industry, but also in fundamentally challenging and changing the rules of the game, it takes a tightly focused and strongly oriented operation. DLI would pass on both counts.

But what has made its real difference in the marketplace is the tightly fashioned way in which DLI manages its staff. Each staff member has become an incredibly productive component in the overall DLI system.

The information collectors

DLI are big fans of information: collecting it, analyzing it and using it to competitive advantage. Chris Smyth, call-center manager for DLI, advises that organizations getting into the telemarketing sector should start by examining the data that is already located in most telephone systems. There is a wealth of information waiting out there that can help the company benchmark future activity by determining work-flows and planning for peaks and troughs of call patterns – as Smyth asks:

> *"If the work volumes in your call center fluctuate what do you do with the staff in quiet times?"*[2]

Idle staff time clearly poses a productivity issue. But idle time also presents the staff with an opportunity to "slip loose" of the tight and productivity oriented environment.

Anatomy of a call-center

In the power donut, the artificial light was pivotal in the information flow between supervisor and inmate. This information flow underpinned the governance of the inmate. In the call-center, the function of the light is performed by the automated call distributor (ACD). The ACD boasts the following features:

1   handles many call at the same time

2   automatically searches out the next available operator

3   plays "holding messages"

4   handles transfer to other sites

5   produces management information

6   has "supervisor" screens so activity of all operators can be monitored in real time.

The ACD can be seen to be a key tool for DLI. Without it, one is merely transferring a face-to-face service to a telephone-based one. As the latter is more impersonal, this would appear initially to be a disadvantage. It certainly could be when it comes to selling financial services if the interface between customer and operator is not rigidly managed. Features 5 and 6 of the ACD, above, are particularly apposite to our discussion here. In the Taylorite mould, information management is the basis for the management not only of the business but also of the people. The following box, produced by DLI, shows (in a fashion that would not have disheartened Taylor) how to plan the staffing of a call center.

> ### How many staff?
>
> | | |
> |---|---|
> | Expected number of calls | × |
> | Average call length | = |
> | Total hours | ÷ |
> | (say) 35 hours | = |
> | Full time equivalents | + |
> | Inefficiency factor | = |
> | Total staff required | |
> | + supervisory staff | |

DLI defines the "inefficiency factor" as time in which the operators will not be working: sickness, holidays, training and estimate it as between 15 and 20 percent.

The ACD can help determine the information needed to fill out the calculations above and to assess ongoing productivity performance when the system is in operation.

Secondly, there is the Taylorite management of the operator–customer interaction. DLI has a series of "tight," "loose" and "mixed" scripts in order to help each operator manage the customer. Selection of script depends on the experience and technical knowledge of the operator as well as the type of customer. DLI does not appear to have a concern that the use of scripts imposes an overly rigid structure on the operator. It is concerned that oversubscribing to the script method might sound "false." What people want is sincerity – and if you can fake that you can fake anything! DLI tends to use scripts like stabilizers on a bicycle – i.e. to get the trainees started.

The "looser" types of script involve what is termed "call patterns" – slotting the caller into classic types for which a prescribed approach is recommended but still maintaining aspects of the tight script, e.g. the "corporate welcome."

The game

- ◆ Why are call-centers so good at delivering higher productivity?
- ◆ Is there a connection between the arrangement of workers in a call-center and 'battery-style' agriculture, e.g. chickens?
- ◆ What is the link between a regimented space and control systems?
- ◆ Is your office an expression of or a reflection of your power? (If both, which has primacy?)

| Thesis | Roles | Aim | Power-principle | Pay-off |

What does the game seem to be about?
The call-center game (CCG) is set up between the two poles of "boredom" and "boredom relief." It could be articulated as "look we know this is a bit of a boring job and we do have to make the numbers, so why don't we try and have a little fun with it ..."

Boredom. DLI acknowledges that the nature of the work is "repetitive and pressured." The organization of the work-space is self-consciously old-fashioned, class room style. Each employee is slotted into the "rabbit hutch" system. The work is regulated, with defined times of start and finish. The average number of calls expected is designed to maintain a constant level of productivity.

The actual way in which each employee deals with a customer is also set out with clearly defined entry and exit points of the conversation, e.g. the "corporate welcome."

The work is repetitive with clearly identified patterns and procedures for each employee to follow. The scope for individual creative contribution is negligible. Even the scope for physical movement while working is extremely limited as each operator works with telephone and screen in a regimented fashion.

Boredom relief, i.e. fun, diversion, distraction or what DLI terms "motivation" breaks down into:

- pay and benefits
- surroundings
- lively and fun
- socials.

Having deliberately set up an alienating workplace configuration, DLI then encourages the employees to break the rules – to subvert aspects of the organizing principles. Remember, call-centers are generally situated in large open-plan spaces with hundreds of operators working at screens, rather like those 1950 and 1960s images of typing pools. But employees are permitted and encouraged to individualize their own work spaces.

Although each employee is isolated in their own individual "hutch" and forms a separate and distinct relation with the central powers by virtue of the technology (ACD), they are also encouraged to form informal bonds of friendship with each other; to take work relations into "social" situations.

This in fact goes further, as DLI not only tolerates but encourages the series of running practical jokes in the office environment, all in the name of breaking the tedium.

Now there is nothing inherently wrong or duplicitous in making life for the employee base as interesting as possible. Making the work day stimulating keeps a level of motivation current within the workforce. But the relief of boredom is part of the game – a game which, as we will see, has control and compliance at its heart. The game thesis is set up using an arid spatial workplace with regimented and rigorous systems. This regimented system is then periodically undermined through boredom relief. Together, the two opposing aspects of boredom and boredom relief set up satisfactory and quantifiable levels of productivity. But how and why? The why is easy.

Productivity is particularly important and key to success for DLI, as part of its new customer offering, when entering the marketplace, was considerably reduced premiums for their financial services. And as with all price-sensitive scenarios – high productivity, and continued gain in market share volume is particularly key to ongoing success.

Let's move on to get the answer to the "how."

| Thesis | **Roles** | Aim | Power-principle | Pay-off |

What is the role of each player?

Four-hander, in which both the management and the employees play two roles each – to match off two levels in action. We could call these the *official* and the *unofficial* sets of roles.

Official

1 *Employee* as worker. He is productive, entering willingly into the system, following the scripts and maintaining pre-agreed call levels. He is aware that there is constant call monitoring but remains a conscious (and perhaps even willing) object in the power relationship set up by the management.

2 *Employer*. He is present but invisible because he maintains the technology and assimilates the information provided by the ACD. The ACD system in some ways acts as a sign for the possible presence of the employer. Remember the way in which the power donut light worked? It indicated the possible (but not certain) presence of the supervisor. The ACD can monitor real productivity in real time. The telephone equipment installed by DLI can allow the supervisor

to "listen in" at any point in the conversations that the workers are conducting.

Again, remember that the telephone calls in these work instances are not just an adjunct to the work carried out by the employee as with many cases. They *are* the work carried out by the employee. The ACD and ancillary technology provide the management with the tools needed for a sophisticated and irrefutable means for establishing and maintaining an extremely high degree of control over the worker.

Unofficial

3 *Employee* as subversive. He enters willingly into the fun of the office games and running practical jokes. He participates in the office "socials" and is a participant in a network of employee relations, sanctioned but formally unrecognised by the management.

4 *Employer* as visible floor manager. He is benevolent, tolerant, motivating. He walks the floors, keen the get the successful call rations up. He cares about the welfare of the staff but is also aware of the other "absent role" signified by the ACD. The ACD constantly calculates productivity and furnishes him with the details he needs for extra attention – e.g. falling call-rate, below expectation customer-courtesy, and so forth.

Thesis	Roles	**Aim**	Power-principle	Pay-off

What is the overall purpose of the game?

Control and compliance. The aim of the game is to create the conditions necessary to effect the "pay-off" – and here that aim is quite clearly control over the employees. And as we have seen, the level of control, as revealed in the analysis of the "anatomy of the call-center" is extreme.

DLI describes the overall principle driving a successful call-center

- but there cannot be fun without control!
- basic disciplines, e.g. time keeping, low sickness, dress standards, etc.
- objectives, e.g. number of calls per day, average call length, number of sales/registrations per day, etc.

- call monitoring – benefit of a call-center is that calls can be listened to and taped
- feedback taped calls to operators breaking down the call in detail and suggesting improvements.

The tools in which DLI has invested allow it near absolute control over each employee as they carry out their duties. No wonder DLI can feel confident when the practical jokes commence that there will not be a lowering of productivity. If there is, the invisible manager will know it instantly; know where it has occurred; whether it is a repeat pattern; whether it needs to be rectified immediately or whether it can be allowed to ride. This information may be then passed onto the visible (floor) manager.

Finally, we can witness in the call-center the ultimate power-base consolidation – the internalizing of the power relations; each employee's knowledge that such information is readily available to the supervisor; the possibility that this actual call in which the operator is engaged *could actually be in the process of being recorded and listened into* – necessitates that each operator effectively governs himself. This makes the employees do their own governing.

Thesis / Roles / Aim / **Power-principle** \ Pay-off

Which is the dominant principle: belief or fear?
Fear (i.e. of the absent supervisor, the ever-present possibility of supervisor intrusion and subsequent sanction). Belief (in the corporate mission) should never be dismissed altogether. But belief will play a subsidiary part in how the power relations are created and maintained.

Thesis / Roles / Aim / Power-principle / **Pay-off** \

What are the ulterior motives?
High productivity. Without the "ulterior motives" – that is, without the distinction between surface-level and real-level aims – we would only be dealing with a set of operations designed to gain an end and therefore not really a true "game." The "thesis" of the CCG game was organized between the polarities of "boredom" and "boredom relief." Power was not

explicit. In this sense, the set-up of the surface-play involved the DLI management setting up an arid work scenario and then encouraging the workforce to subvert parts of it.

But *the ulterior motive, that which is concealed, is extreme control. But why concealed?*

Simply because the naked expression of the control would not in itself yield up the aim of "high productivity" that is sought for. Visible and extreme forms of management will get compliance but not necessarily high productivity or staff retention. Similarly, the mere interplay between boredom and boredom relief would not yield up the high productivity either.

But both scenarios, set up as the apparent "thesis" and the real intent (pay-off) of the CCG game do.

Summary of the call-center game

Thesis
What does the game seem to be about?
Boredom set up and boredom broken

Roles
What is the role of each player?
- Employee as willing object of extreme power relations
- Employee as subversive
- Employer as signified by the ACD technology – not fully visible
- Employer as fully visible "coach"

Aim
What is the overall purpose of the game?
To ensure total employee compliance.

Power-principle
Which is the dominant principle: belief or fear?
Fear; belief.

Pay-off
What are the ulterior motives?
High and sustained levels of productivity

In the CCG, the sophistication of the technology *individualizes* the power relations, e.g. the supervisor can hone in on a specific operator and monitor his/her individual performance against specific and perhaps individually agreed targets. In this sense, the barriers that existed between inmates in the power donut also exist here. This time they are virtual and produced by the technology, but no less potent for that.

In the call-center, there is no gameplan that the workers can agree among themselves, no axis that can be formed, no coalition bonded that can refute the absolute and individual information and power granted to the supervisor.

The call-center space may to some extent resemble the stereotypical dehumanizing work spaces we know from earlier this century (1950s typing pools). However, the space here has also become a constant reminder to the workers of the advanced power relations in operation, almost like one of those signs that says "danger – high voltage!"

But what about the other side of the coin? What about that other modern phenomenon – working from home, teleworking? Perhaps this is a work system that liberates rather than constrains the employee?

THE TELEWORKING GAME

The scene

Working from home – a release from the power donut?

At first glance, this space would seem to be the opposite of the call-center when it comes to the power relationship between employer and employee. The worker from home is in control of his/her own individual space. After all, he/she has chosen where to live, what it looks like, where to work within that space, and quite often exactly when to work. The space in which the personal identity of the individual is both expressed and reflected can be strongest in the home ("Home is where the heart is"). After all it is a home and not a house, which is space plus value. If the call-center represents that space which can be so easily manipulated by the management to leverage its power over you, then surely the opposite set of power dynamics are in action in the home: the space which is yours legally and socially?

For example, technology proved to be the main enabler producing and maintaining the power relations in the call-center and the organization of space key to establishing the "thesis" of the game. In the home, the teleworker has considerably more influence over what technology gets installed and to what end. The teleworker also has more control over the organization of space: He chooses whether to "permit" meetings in his/her own work space and so forth.

Some recent research[3] looks at the reasons behind why many opt for home working in the first place, starting with:

• Reduced need for travel	50%
• Improved quality of working life	42%
• High quality of work possible	29%
• High volume of work possible	21%
• Flexibility of hours/work methods	16%
• Easier child care arrangements	5%

With these specific aims in mind, the research largely showed that teleworking works out successfully, with over 50% claiming that their objectives were fulfilled either well or fully. Additionally, some three-quarters of those surveyed felt that teleworking led to an increase in their own perceived levels of effectiveness.

However, as the researchers note:

> *"A protective barrier between home and work has been removed – protective against the spillover of problems from one domain to the other. The research shows that there is a considerable build up in home related stress experience by those teleworkers surveyed: some 40% report home related stress to be either worse or much worse. Other reported sources of stress were 'working to tight deadlines and timescales;' 'general work overload.'"*[4]

In analyzing the latter point, the researchers note:

> *"Management may even set higher targets for homeworkers in the belief that this is necessary to prevent homeworkers having it too easy, or homeworking being a soft option."*[5]

The issue of target-setting is a critical one is assessing how the adjustment of space (which home working actually is) affects the power relations.

The game

> ◆ Working from home – is that the same as 'free range' for chickens – have you broken out of the coop?
> ◆ Does working from home end up corrupting the home with work-related issues?
> ◆ Can the company still "efficiently" control the employee even though he is no longer within the regimented space of the office?

| **Thesis** | Roles | Aim | Power-principle | Pay-off |

What does the game seem to be about?

The thesis of the teleworking game (TG) is set up between the worker as a subject (i.e. fully himself) and as object (just a cog in the work wheel). The traditional set-up is that home is where we can most be ourselves. Work is where we "sell" ourselves (become an object that is traded). We do so in return for money, status and satisfaction as the main factors. The thesis of the game says:

> *"Look, forget this old-fashioned us and them model. We are both too grown up for that. We, as your employers, recognize that if we give you back more of what you are selling us (i.e. yourself) it will actually work better for both of us. It will be a win–win situation. We trust you to take your work out of its usual place and perform it at home. We hope you will trust us that you still are a key member of the team although you will be at the office much less."*

But of course there exists a real dilemma for the employee: The home (where the employee gets his sense of person) is now also the place where he carries out his masters' bidding.

The dilemma? The employee will continually strive towards but never be able to achieve the level of personal identity because the workplace has now corrupted his home-place.

Again:

> *"A protective barrier between home and work has been removed – protective against the spillover of problems from one domain to the other."*[6]

This is stressful for the employee, stressful in the sense that there are two contrary impulses at play: the need to gain subjectivity – as symbolized and constantly prompted by the home; and the need to retain a relationship with the employer – and therefore admitting a degree of reification (dehumanization) and maintaining "object" status.

A case in point: when scientists want to stress rats in the laboratory, they send two contrary impulses. For example: the buzzer sounds and the rat goes to the trough where food is dispensed. The light in the corner flashes on and the rat receives an electric shock whenever it touches the trough. It associates the buzzing sound with food and the flashing light with pain.

What does the rat do the following week when, a regular pattern having been established, the flashing light signifies food available in the trough and the buzzer brings with it a shock? It gets stressed!

In the same way, the employee has his reminder of home all around him. Why shouldn't he? That is where he is. But he now also has the trappings of work because that is what he needs to perform.

Like the confused rat, the employee has two contrary impulses going on, which leads to stress. And as indicated earlier, the research shows a reported 40% of those surveyed considered home-related stress to be worse or much worse.

In short, the thesis of the game is set up as an opposition between

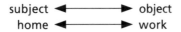

and the constant attempt to reconcile the dilemma.

Thesis / **Roles** \ Aim \ Power-principle \ Pay-off

What is the role of each player?

Three-hander.

- *Employee* as home worker: He tries to reconcile the contrary impulses drawing him along the subject-object or home-work axis.
- *Employer* as absent: He is able to manipulate at a distance. He tightly manages both of the employee outputs from home and will also manage the information flow towards the employee. As with the call-center, the employee is much less able to tap into the unofficial network of information flows normally open to the employee. To this extent the employer is able to "narrow-band"[7] the relationship.

  In other words, he can contract and focus the information which goes from the company to the employee. The shotgun is replaced with a rifle!

- *Family:* They have to support the employee's "to-ing" and "fro-ing" along the subject-object axis. They are also in the paradoxical position of having to support the work environment and try also to exclude it. As one respondent in the survey observed:

  > *"They (i.e. the office) have our private number, and many times they call on it, as if by mistake ..."[8]*

Thesis / **Roles** / **Aim** \ Power-principle \ Pay-off

What is the overall purpose of the game?

Control. At the surface level the employee is much more empowered than our friend located in the call-center. It would appear that he or she is able to dictate much more of the agenda than the call-center employees.

Additionally, management control is relegated to the outputs rather than the process – another clear distinction. However, there are significant elements of similarity with both the teleworker and the inmates of the *Power Donut*.

Here is a brief summary of what the teleworker has in common with the call-center operator:

- Each is separated from his fellow worker and therefore individualized by the narrow-banding (contracting) of the organization; the narrow-banding both channels the outgoing information about organizational activities to the employee AND contracts the basis for assessing employee largely to the output. This in turn changes the employer-employee relationship from a task-oriented to a person-oriented transaction (a hallmark of the command and control management style).
- The employee has to become his own effective governor in place of the absent employer. In this sense the power-relations are internalised similar to that which takes place for the call-center operators and the inmate in the *Power Donut*.

The question posed at beginning of this section was posed as: "Working from home – release from the power donut?" As we have seen, the tactics of individualizing the employee and internalizing the power relations result in an effective and advanced form of exercise of power.

Whereas the bars of the cell were real as envisaged by Jeremy Bentham,[9] in the call-center they are virtual (produced by the operation of the ACD).

The bars for the teleworker are psychological, for he is controlled at a distance by the manager. Working from home only creates an illusory release from the power donut.

For the teleworker, the fact remains that the mechanisms for control and command have been transplanted internally (and supported by the organizational mechanisms for specifically assessing the output of the employee), by:

- individualizing the employee, i.e. abstracting him/her from the unofficial network of alliances with others
- contracting (narrowbanding)the amount of information that goes towards the individual
- corrupting the place for the self (the home) and locking the employee into an unending journey back and forth along the subject–object axis.

| Thesis | Roles | Aim | **Power-principle** | Pay-off |

Which is the dominant principle: belief or fear?

Belief (in the corporate proposition or the company line). The official organizational "propaganda" becomes increasingly important and key to sustaining the individual as it assumes a higher position than unofficial networked information. The company line is increasingly all that the teleworker has to go on and cling to.

Fear can enter, but at a lower level than belief and certainly lower than the fear levels in the call-center. Fear here would only manifest itself as fear of being sidelined; of not knowing what is being planned; of being alienated from the decision-making powers (or being peripheral to the center). In this sense the fear is not pure fear – it is "unbelief" (an inverted form of belief): a realization that the corporate proposition as handed out might be a ruse and that to which he is clinging an illusion.

| Thesis | Roles | Aim | Power-principle | **Pay-off** |

What are the ulterior motives?

Productivity. The research showed that one of the recurring reasons for the reported stress included "working to tight deadlines and timescales" and "general work overload." The research even speculates that the management of home-workers might even be setting higher targets for them. If you count commuting time as dead time or at least reduced potential working time, then homeworking can present real productivity gains, with a narrow focus on measurable employee outputs. According to the research, the time saved on commuting is as follows:

Less than 1 hour per homeworking day	22.6%
1–2 hours per homeworking day	35.5%
2–3 hours per homeworking day	22.6%
3+ hours per homeworking day	19.3%

Summary of the teleworking game

Thesis

What does the game seem to be about?
Journey towards a greater appreciation and utilization of the self.

Roles

What is the role of each player?
- Employee – journeying towards full realisation of the self but now condemned to also be an object (unit of productivity) in the work system.
- Employer – he sets objective performance measures from a distance. He intrudes into the employee home by a number of means.
- Family – companion to the employee; context for the realization of self by the employee; corrupted by the employer.

Aim

What is the overall purpose of the game?
Control.

Power-principle

Which is the dominant principle: belief or fear?
Belief; fear.

Pay-off

What are the ulterior motives?
High and sustained levels of productivity.

The discussion

Niccolo seems satisfied. "All this talk about empowerment is all very fine and often quite key to the success of the enterprise – as long as you do not forget two things. Firstly, the question of empowering the employee only enters at the level of 'thesis' – that it is a maneuver that conceals a real set of transactions. Secondly, the aim of the enterprise is about securing owner value – and the employees can help deliver that value but we must logically minimize their subsequent claim on that value. If you want to accrue power for yourself you must first learn how to break free of these current power relations in which (as an employee) you find yourself.

I interjected: "I feel a little uncomfortable with how ... cold all of this is. We are dealing with real people, real employees not some theoretical inmates of a 19th-century jail."

Niccolo replied: "Do not misunderstand me – the employees are vital to success but only as pawns in the game. And like pawns they are expendable in the quest for success. From the employer's perspective, the secret is how to ensure that they do his bidding and that means slotting them into a power relationship that will ensure their malleability. If you are somewhat uneasy about this whole process, then perhaps you should take up a more noble pursuit?

"But you cannot treat people like this in the late 20th century! We will not tolerate it – this is not a situation where you could sack people at will and make them work in large sweat-houses," I replied

"What has changed, my dear fellow," replied Niccolo, "all lies at the level of the game 'thesis'. The thesis will adapt to changing conditions, ideologies and methods of working. However, the real pay-off of the business game – higher yields – can still only be secured through efficient power relations. I agree you cannot treat people in the 20th century like you could in the 19th, or the 16th century for that matter.

"That does not mean you change your whole approach. It does mean that you modulate the inner workings of the game to arrive at a system which is going to achieve the task."

"Are you saying that you just change the words – but keep the real modus operandi *the same?" I asked.*

"In some ways yes, but this is not just about rhetoric versus reality. The rhetoric makes the reality. But you are not a philosopher and I shall not bore you with philosophical musings. However, we should take note of how a 'strategic' approach to 'managing' the employee space links into managing the relationship between the employer and employee. We should also not forget that both the call-center and teleworking are modern-day phenomena – and look set to engage more and more employees in the years ahead. You initial task is to understand how, as an employee, you are locked into a power relationship with the organization. In time, when you take on the mantle of power, you will also use these same tactics to maintain control over your subordinates. Your next task – as set out in the technology game – is to look to subvert or break the hold that the organization has over you. This will then allow you to move towards being able to wield power for yourself and ultimately for your corporation."

Notes

1   F. Taylor, *The Principles of Scientific Management* (Dover Publications, 1998).
2   Chris Smyth, *Anatomy of a Call-Center*, presentation by Direct Line (1998).
3   Y. Baruch and N. Nicholson, "Home, sweet work: requirements for effective home working," *Journal of General Management* (1997).
4   *Ibid.*
5   *Ibid.*
6   *Ibid.*
7   A term that came up in conversation with Professor Paul Willman of London Business School.
8   Baruch and Nicholson.
9   M. Foucault, *Discipline and Punish*.

Breaking Power

THE TECHNOLOGY GAME

The scene

"Over time, tension will grow, pitting the global world of digital commerce and online society against the more local worlds of traditional governments and of people who aren't part of the 'brave new world.'"

Esther Dyson[1]

Dyson frames the fight in regulatory terms. But regulation comes after the dust has settled. Regulation consolidates the position of the winner. The winner is still far from clear. In this next round of *The Power Game*, we look at how the *cyber-age* can break the hold the corporation has over the individual. This in turn will allow him to break free and begin to wield power on his own or on the corporation's behalf. That the cyber-age actually poses a issue for the corporation in terms of power relations has first to be established.

Up until now much discussion about information management has focused on how the corporation can enhance performance using new technologies (Federal Express – parcel tracking using the Internet); or on product innovation (Mondex Electronic Purse – electronic cash); or on how new competitors have changed the rules of the game and over-turned dominant players (Amazon.com – Internet book shop).

But the real impact of new technology on the corporation promises to be more fundamental as it will involve a profound struggle. This battle will be between those who have power (the corporation) and those who have increasing access to information, thereby dissipating that power. The opponents reside outside the corporate boundary: consumers, po-tential consumers, trade customers, shareholders, competitors, regula-tors and activists.

The cozy coterie that the average multi-million pound corporation can command (lobbyists, lawyers, scientists, spin-doctors, trade asso-ciations) is threatened in this "brave new world." The cohesive, consis-tent voice and face of the corporation will be shattered and with it the power which it has so carefully nurtured and enhanced.

Back to the power donut

In the first chapter we saw how the manipulation of space could control the flow of information, internalize the power relations (making them more efficient) and maintain a productive power relationship between the supervisor and inmate. Space played a key role, for it fixed the in-mate. It allowed the construction of an information transaction that not only maintained the power-relationship but actually helped create it.

The inmates were separated from each other and unable to form alli-ances of any value. They all received pre-packaged information from the centre while offering up near total information about themselves.

Up until now, the corporation has been able to maintain its power status through the management of information inside and outside of its borders. When it comes to its employees, the activist groups and the media generally, the corporation could maintain and perhaps gain in-fluence in key areas (marketplace; factory-floor; AGMs) through privi-leged access to information.

The corporate advantage lay in the ability to source and disseminate (where "appropriate") information more quickly and more accurately than its foes. But what is the impact on the power relations if the humble individual can get hold of the same information with equal speed and ease?

The "threat" of technology lies in its ability to end "representationalism"

In many respects, the cyber-age poses a greater threat to corporate power than those other antagonists such as the activist groups – because the threat is amorphous. The threat poses a challenge not only for the corporation but also for other "fixed" institutions of power, which "represent" (i.e. have been invested with/by others to represent) interests on their behalf. In this sense, democracy (getting politicians to *represent* our views), as well as other key social institutions, relies on a representational notion of power. Religion is another classic example in which the priest/institutional representative can represent or make manifest a higher authority to its followers.

In fact, the concept of "representation" is implicit right through *The Power Game*. Employees, activists, media are all part of this chain of investment and representation:

- Employees invest trust, and contributions to their union and are then "represented" – thereby leveraging their collective impact.
- Pressure group members invest their time, organizational powers, beliefs and contributions and are then "represented" by the likes of Greenpeace. Activists represent their membership and leverage their geographical spread and often their active participation when targeting a company or industry sector.
- The media is given permission by the audience (by tuning in/buying a newspaper) to have that particular medium represent the world for it The world becomes the "world according to ..." *The Economist* or *The New York Times*.

In fact the whole democratic process is based on representation. The permission given by the public to politicians to represent their views is partly one of convenience: As Dyson puts it:

> *"Right now politically the United States is in a sorry state. Only 49 per cent of the potential voters bothered to vote in the most recent presidential elections ... People are rational, and they know that one person's vote won't change the outcome.*

Others feel a certain social responsibility, and so they vote any-
way. But voting does not make a real democracy, any more
than taxes are an expression of philanthropy."[2]

Aside from convenience, this issue of representationalism as we have seen is also clearly involved in a power transaction. The people delegate power upward and are then told what do to. In some ways, this is a similar "shape" of transaction to the interplay in the power donut. It took belief or fear within the inmate to set the scene whereby the supervisor gained and maintained a position of power.

Let us remember that it was not just a coercive relationship – i.e. the inmate was motivated by the fear of being seen by the supervisor, or fear of the retaliatory measures. There was a second operating principle: one of belief, whereby the inmate not only believed that he was being watched (which is really fear) but also perhaps believed in the system or the reality that placed him within that structure in the first place. This is exactly the same belief that maintains the democratic power relations.

In the power donut, the supervisor was symbolized or represented by the light. In the Cyber-age, the ways in which third party bodies or institutions represent the interests of the individual are changing radically and will continue to do so.

Governments can no longer be out of touch with the varying demands of the population. The Labour Government in the UK, under the leadership of Blair, constantly polls the population in order to keep sensitizing its messages and policies:

"Via Gould's small clusters of voters, Labour has been asking
the public how it should smarten up: whether pistachio or red
is the right colour for party conferences, whether 'toughness'
towards crime is a good policy to highlight.
*   "The process has been couched in neutral, pragmatic terms*
– 'getting in touch with the real world' is the way Gould's allies
most often describe it – yet, by 'listening' to voters so hard and
for so long, the Party may have changed its substance as much
as its image."[3]

Religion in many parts of the world has lost its role of being "representative" of a higher power and getting used to being on the periphery of secular society, losing influence on traditional policy strongholds such as health, education and even public morality. Religion is becoming just another voice in the chorus-line, another color in the kaleidoscope.

In many respects, the falling trust or interest in government (49% is a very low figure for a nation that prides itself on its democratic processes) is also visible in the rise of the activist group. The reason why pressure groups such as Greenpeace are able to command such attention and goodwill among their memberships is that it they occupy a space in the public trust zone vacated by government.

Greenpeace is therefore *invested* with some power to *represent* interests and there is a consequent falling off of power within the government. As the German author Heiden remarked: "Unused power slips imperceptibly into the hands of another."

All around us in the age of information, there is dissipation in the traditional modes of representation. This has direct implication for the corporate–public transaction. Let us look at a few situations where the individual (helped by technology) chooses new ways of representing *their own* interests.

When does the revolution start with the monarchy?[4]

Hamel's line suggests that change is always bottom or peripherally driven, never a top-down central initiative. In the same way, the overturn of the corporate dominance will not be driven from within but from without. The individual, through his ability to form meaningful informal alliances, is already forming strong and direct challenges to the corporation.

Remember the teleworking game: the very means of maintaining a powerful corporate grip over the worker lay in the ability to "narrowband" the relationship. This meant keeping a tight control on the information flow going out to the individual employee. The teleworking agreement makes it difficult for the employee to form meaningful alliances with the others. British Telecom teleworkers often meet each other in motorway service stations in order to maintain some informal/unofficial contact with each other.

But it is now clear that the ability for the individual to access information pertinent to his or her own interest is turning the tables.

To demonstrate this simply before moving on to the more complex relationship between the individual and the corporation, let us look at the classic power relations between the patient and the doctor. This is an example of extreme power relations (and therefore a good one). The patient has to offer up total and honest information about his own body to the doctor, the possessor of knowledge. As the great French thinker Foucault wrote:

> "The great asylum physician is both the one who can tell the truth of the disease through the knowledge he has of it ... through the power that his will exerts on the patient himself"[5]

But technology is heralding a new dawn for the patient.

AIDS and the changing doctor–patient power relationship

Foucault tragically died of AIDS-related illnesses in 1984. Let us look at the way technology is now able to inform the suffering patient about this condition and the way in which this information can materially change the patient–doctor power relationship.

The Web allows anyone to access the following kind of information quickly: Just imagine what the availability of the following type of information does to the regular doctor–patient relationship. Now it is the patient who knows the latest clinical trials, who is involved, what the timeline is with regard to availability.

> **"Drug cocktail seems to eliminate HIV where it hides**
> "A new combination of drugs is capable of eliminating all detectable levels of HIV in the body tissues where it is known to reside, researchers say. Previous studies have shown that the drugs can reduce the level of HIV in the bloodstream, but the virus is also known to hide in the tonsils, lymph nodes, spinal fluid, and semen.

> *"Sven Danner, of the University of Amsterdam, and col-*
> *leagues, report that six patients given a combination of Glaxo*
> *Wellcome's AZT and 3TC and Abbott Laboratories' protease*
> *inhibitor Norvir had no sign of HIV in their tonsil tissue after*
> *six months of treatment. A separate study found that the com-*
> *bination of AZT, 3TC, and Boehringer Ingelheim's drug*
> *Viramune had a similar impact on HIV in the lymph tissue of*
> *patients who had no detectable HIV in their blood."*[6]

Or again:

> *"People taking medications for HIV may get discouraged if they*
> *feel sicker after they start a drug treatment than they did be-*
> *fore. They may feel that the quality of their life was better be-*
> *fore starting their drug.* **Talk to your doctor if you feel this**
> **way so you can make an informed decision about your**
> *treatment."*[7] *[my highlights]*

The information which is available one-to-one for the individual is as-
tonishing and it will take a pretty informed doctor to be able to keep up
with his patient. At this point the patient is ceasing to be just a passive
object there to receive the best advice the doctor can provide (at which-
ever point in the information curve he/she is) and thereby take some
power back for him/herself.

This does not just apply to the ability to access information at an
individual level. The Web is more than an electronic library. It is interactive. This allows the individual to form informal alliances, thereby
accruing more and more anecdotal information about his own condition.
This is information that could never normally be gathered by an individual prior to the Internet.

Forming informal alliances: an Internet example

Via wbs.net one can visit the personal sites of and correspond directly
with:

> *4ever a student:*
> Interested in cardiology & Neonatology
> *92163:*
> I am interested in hearing from those with hypothyroidism
> *acute ass:*
> Surgical first assistant
> *BeeEss:*
> I am looking for individuals who have become ill from expo-
> sure to the weedkiller "Roundup"
> *BJL150:*
> I like to keep informed of new medical information
> *chemoRN:*
> I'm an oncology nurse, and mum, and parrothead!
> *Commander-General Adama:*
> I am a chronic asthmatic who enjoys supporting others with
> respiratory illnesses
> *curious the Mighty:*
> Emergency Department RN/manager
> *cwall12:*
> I am a registered Dietician specialising in wellness, diabetes,
> renal nutrition

The Web provides the user with the ability to access information and thereby gain a wealth of information about his/her own condition. It also allows each user to form and be part of a "web" of alliances and information exchanges which can form nodal points outside of and perhaps even antagonistic to the interest of business.

Remember *BeeEss*?

> *"I am looking for individuals who have become ill from expo-
> sure to the weedkiller 'Roundup.'"*

BeeEss doesn't just want to share information on a health basis. It is not absurd to suppose that if the response to BeeEss's message was strong, some formal (legal?) representation to Monsanto (the manufacturers of Roundup) might be ensuing?

This type of information and information network, now available so cheaply to the individual, would never have been possible using traditional forms of research (private detectives/medical searches/trawls of relevant journals) due to both time, financial and educational limitations on the individual.

The corporate challenge

As we saw, the health-care industry is a sector in which to view clearly how the dominant forces (medical profession, pharmaceutical companies) might be challenged effectively and easily through the collection and positioning of information sourced on the Web. This also holds true for the many other commercial spheres.

Let's go to Hollywood

Take the Hollywood film industry a powerful and market-led sector, which is being threatened by Harry Knowles, a single, overweight film-buff who posts film reviews from his bedroom in Austin Texas. The site is called www.aint-it-cool-news.com and seeks to give advance warning on whether an upcoming film release is good or not. It its own words:

> *"Ain't It Cool News is a Harry Knowles production bringing you the latest in movie, TV, comic and other coolness that's got Hollywood's panties in a bunch."*

As Harry describes his own growing fame/infamy, so also the network of informal alliances begins to grow around him:

> *"Wow, here ya are! Well my little site keeps on growing, much to my shock. As you will find I attempt to cover all stages of development of the films that you and I look forward to, without the 'studio line' clouding our judgement.*
>
> *"This site works with the help of people like you. Now everyone has a chance to be a 'spy,' because inevitably at some point there will be a moment where Hollywood enters your life, before it enters ours. If you see something filming, a trailer, an*

advance screening or something I can't even imagine. If you read a script, hear something from behind the scenes ... well let me know. I try to cover it all, and you, your neighbors, boss, or even the local weatherman ... well yall make this site special. It's your eyes, ears and opinions, well ... we're making a difference. Also we do cover the 'uncool' films, we warn each other of the Hollywood powered Nuclear Bombs, and the super cool products."

Note the use of the word "spies." Harry is openly exhorting a show of subversion to the multi-billion dollar Hollywood industry, an industry which test markets its products (particularly its ending) on focus groups, adapting the final product to consumer needs.

Harry's warnings to site users have made him a target of Hollywood vitriol, and some attention.

Quentin Tarantino succumbs to Harry's power

Jackie Brown was the much anticipated offering from film producer/ director/writer/actor Quentin Tarantino, who was responsible for highly successful and "cool" *Pulp Fiction*. *Jackie Brown* was a different product – less reliant on violence, black humor and a stylish soundtrack. Instead it focused on real people caught in a world of small-time crime who have to cope with the growing realization that life is progressing and they have less to show for it. *Jackie Brown* was hailed as a more "mature" film but was receiving mixed reviews from influential critics – far less ecstatic than for *Pulp Fiction*.

Such is the power of Harry Knowles' web site that he and his family were taken out on the town in Austin by Tarantino and his cohorts. Although Harry does not see it as such, such "entertainment" could be viewed as a slick piece of lobbying by Tarantino on behalf of his own film:

"When afterwards I was invited to go out with the group to eat at Kerbey Lane North. So, Dad, RoRo, Felicia and I all went out. I sat at the table with Linklater, Tarantino, Louis Black, Felicia, RoRo and Rodriguez."

Jackie Brown receives a glowing account by Harry on his site. It has (like *Pulp Fiction*) been formally accepted into the world of "cool."

Such is the enormous investment in films that a few failures can threaten the financial health of the studio. This makes powerful media such as *aint-it-cool-news* absolutely key in determining how the weather vane of popular opinion will swing. Harry has been keen to distance himself from the commercial interests that might influence the more mainstream reviewers. He stresses that the banner advertising in his site (the movie review section is currently sponsored by Sprint) is unsolicited, does not influence him and has the benefit of keeping the site free of charge to users.

The game

- If knowledge equals power, and information leads to knowledge, then can information delivery mechanisms (such as the Internet) lead to a change in the power-levels of the user?
- Will corporates ever fully tame the Internet?
- Why does the Web always have an air of the subversive about it?

| Thesis | Roles | Aim | Power-principle | Pay-off |

What does the game seem to be about?

In breaking down and analyzing the components of the technology game, we must look at the question of agency, i.e. who is behind the technological revolution? Who is behind the explosion of information that is freely available.

The history of the Web shows us that business did *not* start the Web, but business has now desperately been trying to catch up and to exploit the potential.

"E-commerce estimated at $8 billion in 1997 is predicted to jump to an astonishing $333 billion by the year 2002 which is equivalent to 1% of the global economy."[8]

Yet intranets (internal corporate sites) still lag behind the sophistication of Internet sites. Many Web-based businesses have yet to turn a real dollar (including Amazon.com). The point being that if you are looking for the agent in the technology revolution, it will probably be somewhere outside the corporate boundary.

The flow of people onto the net has not been created by the technology industry but facilitated by it. The cost of PCs, software and telephony has made for ease of use, which creates the right conditions. But the impetus for the profusion of net usage also lies in a growing distrust of the primary bodies who would seek to represent us and (if the power donut setup is valid) those who would also wish to separate us from one another.

The Internet revolution has been started by all of us

The agents are each and every one of the Web surfers who are reaching out into cyberspace looking for information, for virtual contact, for a cyber-community, for an alternative point of view.

The thesis of the game revolves around the desire to put oneself and one's own opinion center stage: to cease being just an object (of marketing, for example) and become a subject in a dialog unrestricted by censorship, national mores, or religious hang-ups.

In some way, the use of the Web is not indicative of a desire just for information. We have more information than we will ever need. The babbling of the Internet is an attempt by the individual to claw power back. In this electronic graffiti, we can witness humanity striving for a connection. As we cross the psychological threshold of the new millennium, this is what will pass for meaning.

Corporate graffiti[9]

This electronic graffiti is writing on the wall for the way in which the corporate presence expresses and manifests itself in our society. The huge and growing cyber-community is made up of a proliferating network of alliances, which have little real care for the business. Indeed, they are theoretically opposed to powerful bodies, government/religious institutions, corporations, etc. In the case of www.aint-it-cool-news.com, Harry Knowles seeks to provide his audience with honest and unadulterated reviews, free from the influences of the Hollywood marketing machine.

The corporation (Korean Air) gets bypassed

Another example: in August of 1997, Korean Air Flight 801 crashed, killing 225 people. On CNN Interactive, the message boards were buzzing with experts commenting; with eyewitness descriptions; with surfers speculating.

The official channels of communication – government, airline company, assembled media – were all providing conflicting observations and opinions on what happened.

CNN Interactive was one of the sites where many went to share a "truer," less hysterical or defensive and self-interested version of exactly what happened.

As one surfer put it:

> *"The news media seems to have difficulty in getting the details of aviation accidents correct. Contrary to many media reports, the glidescope system of the ILS, or instrument landing system, is not a system to guide an airplane at night ..."*
>
> (Tim Serey)

The thesis of the technology game, therefore, is rooted in the will for a more honest or truer picture of things being shared among the cyber-community members. It seeks to subvert or circumvent the official channels (bolstered by its relative freedom from libel laws) and celebrate its unofficial and "free" status. The thesis in summary:

> *"I am entitled to as much information about the world around me as possible and free of charge. The Web is the key tool to help me make that happen. It also allows me to share that information with a new global community with similar interests and without constraint."*

| Thesis | **Roles** | Aim | Power-principle | Pay-off |

What is the role of each player?

A simple "us and them" two-hander: "us" being the surfers; "them" being the regulators who might want to constrain information sharing – corporations who just want to commercialize the Web are also included.

1   Them

The net-heads who champion freedom of speech, privacy and the radical democracy. The Web environment has up until now and perhaps always will have an air of the "unofficial." This is manifest most simply in the sense that there is very little *original* corporate material produced for the Web.

Most of the content of the corporate site is at best tailored electronic versions of materials that have existed in different formats. Companies, particularly in Europe, are still struggling to find the right Web "register," i.e. tone of voice. This is partly to do with the newness of the medium and the requirement to replace static one-directional communications with dynamic interactive ones.

It has also got to do with the difficulty in reconciling the official corporate voice of the organization with the inherently anarchic and self-debunking nature of the medium. Of course, at its most tedious, the corporation tries to use the medium as an electronic shop window. An easy comparison can be seen with HMV (http://www.hmv.co.uk/), essentially an online version of a hard-copy sales brochure. Contrast this with cdnow.com, in which you can sample the music of the artist, the album and place an immediate order in a simple and efficient manner.

The Internet is pornographic. The huge amount of pornography available on the Internet is also testimony to the inherently secretive, "alternative" appeal of the medium. Pornography is that which is rejected by society. It occupies a place beyond the line of social respectability and what is considered the normal interplay between humans. Many bemoan the amount of pornography on the Internet and would attempt to have it cleaned up. But that is to miss the point.

The *nature* of the medium is inherently "pornographic." The role of "them" in the technology game is the role of the "liberated" – free from the constraints endured by "us."

One of the most consistent threats to the Clinton administration has been the *Drudge Report* – which Brill's Content[10] describes as a "flamboyantly provocative, often outrageous Internet news compendium that is roiling the elite journalistic establishment all the way to the president of the United States." Clinton allegedly calls it the Sludge Report! In one month alone, following his breaking of the Monica Lewinsky story, the Drudge site received over 6 million visits – 29,000 from the White House.

2 Us

With every outside, peripheral, subversive or unofficial, there has to be an insider; a normative, an official. The former category gets its meaning from the latter. The Internet subverts the role normally played by the local social order (us).

The local rules of governance are replaced or displaced by the anonymous and mischievous surfer who threatens the "collective standards of moral order." In a business environment, the Internet threatens to throw out not only the rules of the game but the whole game itself. Businesses that took years to form, building trade, customer relations, quality assurance and the like, see three-year-old organizations float for billions of dollars on the exchange. Look at the speed at which Java built up a customer base. It just does not make any sense in a normal business model. And the scale of the wealth means that we are not just looking at upstarts who will disappear tomorrow.

How can you control the nature of a Web product? How can you tax? How can you enforce local laws when the business is Internet-based. How, for example, can an individual state in the US in which gambling is prohibited stop online casinos?

The technology game's second role, that of "us," is one which most of us play most of the time. We do this by paying taxes, fulfilling regulatory criteria, being regular citizens. By doing so, we perpetuate the social and commercial principles that the Internet culture rejoices in subverting.

The citizens of the cyber-communities would view everyday existence as one that is tainted and manipulated by the marketers; trammeled in social and commercial orthodoxy and censorship; hung up on the mores of yesteryear. In a word it is the world and the role of the "unfree."

Thesis | Roles | **Aim** | Power-principle | Pay-off
What is the overall purpose of the game?

The aim of the technology game is to create a separate, distinct "cyber-world" in which people can communicate without national, religious or regulatory intervention.

But this is not just merely about creating alternatives. This cyber-world is "pornographic," not just in the literal sense of porn availability. Pornographic also in the sense that part of its function is to subvert accepted norms. The technology game creates not just a different world, which would be "free" in the view of the net-heads. The game also seeks to undermine many normal acts of officialdom. In this sense, the Internet is also inherently revolutionary. From the perspective of personal power, it can break the grip that the corporation places on you (whether you are on the inside or the outside of the organization) and set you on your way to accruing personal power for yourself. If the organization can lock the employee into a power relation by manipulating the space in which he operates; then the Internet displaces this spatial organization and replaces it with virtual space – the first step in liberating and empower-ing the individual.

Thesis | Roles | Aim | **Power-principle** | Pay-off
Which is the dominant principle: belief or fear?

Belief, in the sense that the cyber-world purports values (radical free-dom of speech) asking you (the individual) to subscribe.

Thesis | Roles | Aim | Power-principle | **Pay-off**
What are the ulterior motives?

The thesis of this game round described how the advent of the techno-logical revolution was about sharing information. It was about celebrat-ing freedom and democracy on the Web. It symbolized and also marked the progress of humanity.

But it is really not just about this. It is also, as you see from the "roles" of the game, about subversion and circumvention. In that sense, the real pay-off of the technology game is less innocent than the mere celebration of trans-national communication.

The value that the Internet presents to the individual is summed up in the fact that the corporation is losing control over the information (*about itself and its commercial operations*) that is publicly available.

The marginalized corporation

The Internet facilitates networks of alliances. It allows the individual to represent him/herself, directly taking power into his/her own hands. Isolated pieces of the jigsaw are put together to form bigger pictures. These pictures allow the individual to begin to break the corporate grip and begin the journey towards accruing power and knowledge for him/herself.

On the CNN Interactive message board[11] after the Guam crash, Korean Air, the media and the Government were all ignored as possible or credible sources of information. Some samples:

> *"It is not surprising that the Korean media has quickly jumped on the 'bad weather' and 'landing system' as likely causes to this tragedy ..."*
>
> (Tom Serey)
>
> *"I could see the crash from my house the night it happened ... I am proud to say that the efforts of both the military and civilians here on Guam has been nothing short of amazing ..."*
>
> (William H Shaw III)
>
> *"At 3 miles from the runway, the course of the jumbo jet should be in the final approach position or on the centre of the runway. So the most probable cause of the crash is due to pilot error."*
>
> (mdk.vic)
>
> *"I am a Captain for a major US airline ... My greatest disappointment is reserved for the hyena-like activities of your journalists mercilessly hounding the bereaved ..."*
>
> (Rory Kay)

The corporate reputations of tomorrow will increasingly be determined by message boards such as these. Victims, eyewitnesses, experts, commentators and gossips will all share information and opinion without corporate blessing or involvement. Korean Air's own version of events, its own safety record, its reassurance to its customers – none of these items made it onto these message boards.

The pay-off for the net-heads lies in the circumvention of the corporate stance and the subversion of the corporate values. This will then allow them to establish distinct power-bases. The central light in the *Power Donut* gets shattered and the power-base of the organization is radically challenged.

Summary of the technology game

Thesis
What does the game seem to be about?
We all have a right to share and access as much information as is out there – that can only be a good thing.

Roles
What is the role of each player
1   Them
2   Us.

Aim
What is the overall purpose of the game?
Wildly democratic sharing of information.

Power-principle
Which is the dominant principle: belief or fear?
Belief.

Pay-off
What are the ulterior motives?
Subversion and marginalization of the social and corporate order; the emergence of a new personal power-base.

The discussion

I was eager to get started: "I thought technology could be used to maintain power relations such as in the case of the call-centre, not to break power relations."

"Indeed yes," replied Niccolo, "the power base will lie with those who can establish the most relevant information base. In the case of the call-centre, it was the absent manager with the assistance of the technology who presided over the information base. The radical democratization of information now means that most, with varying intentions, can gain considerable intelligence about your organization. This essentially leads to a dissipation of the corporate power-base. It is as simple as that. If you want to hold onto that power, you need to hold onto privileged information. If you want to subvert the power of the corporation, then clearly technology is a good thing.

"Indeed all the traditional power-bases, not just commercial, are threatened in the new age we are entering," Niccolo continued.

"But you don't mean to say that the corporations of tomorrow are going to out of business?" I asked.

"No, commercial trading will always continue – but the traditional means by which the organization maintains its owner value will radically alter, and technology will be one of the key factors prompting this. This is because the net will fragment the corporate power base and hand it back to the people."

Niccolo continued: "The struggle in the game is between the official and the unofficial – yes? Between the legitimate corporation and its business operations and the illegitimate subversive Internet?"

"But the Internet is just a thing – it can't do anything of its own accord," I argued

"Well yes – but I also mean the Internet culture, the belief systems that shape the atmosphere of the Web. That is what I intend."

"OK."

Niccolo continued: "This Internet culture shares information, perpetuates truths and rumors. In fact it blurs the difference and treats them with the same respect.

"This is the medium which caused a major crisis for Intel and which

has thousands and thousands of anti-Bill Gates sites and also has en-abled the Drudge Report to be so effective. This is the medium which does not censor the individual voice and which will treat that voice in equal value to the corporate one. The dawn of the Internet also her-alded the birth of the individual power-base."

Notes

1   E Dyson, *Release 2.0: A Design for Living in the Digital Age* (London: Viking, 1997).
2   *Ibid.*
3   *The Guardian*, June 26 1998, p. 2.
4   Strategic thinker Gary Hamel ended most of his presentations in the 1990s with this question.
5   M. Foucault, *Ethics* (London: Allen Lane, 1997).
6   http://www.hivpositive.com/f-Treatment/5-Treatments/f-RTIs/ Hide.html
7   http://www.hivpositive.com/f-Treatment/5-Treatments/ProteaseYou/ prot11.html
8   J. Borzo, *InfoWorld*, Volume 20, p. 78, May 18, 1998.
9   A term coined by Professor Tom Robertson, Goizueta Business School, Atlanta, Georgia.
10   D. McClintick, *Brill's Content*, p. 112, November 1998.
11   http://plus-cgi.cnn.com

Games You Can Play

The pay-rise game

◆ Getting a pay-rise entails that you change the power relations between you and your company

◆ You negotiate your pay-rise based on *future* not past performance

◆ Follow the steps and fill in the exercise – this game will help you plan for and negotiate more money for your endeavors.

Thesis \ Roles \ Aim \ **Power-principle** \ **Pay-off**

What does the game seem to be about?

Identify a "thesis" or key value that will set the game up. For example, in a family-oriented organization* (that which openly espouses family values), take a family-specific thesis such as "I need the extra money to afford a better home for my family, or a better school for my daughter." Be aware that the pay-rise game should never be about you selfishly

---

* To identify the type of company you work for, please see an excellent paper entitled "What Holds the Modern Company Together?" (Rob Gofee and Gareth Jones, *Harvard Business Review*, November–December 1996, pp. 133–148).

wanting more money "because you deserve it." That could set up a local battle between you and your boss, which might get you nowhere. Rather it is about a selfless value such as a home for your family.

Other examples of theses: in a mercenary corporate environment, there might be a premium placed on the company being seen to reward success.

In this instance, the thesis could be set up as "rewarding success." Again, this is not about you getting more money – it is about you providing the company with the opportunity to restate visibly a core value.

Thesis / **Roles** \ Aim \ Power-principle \ Pay-off

What is the role of each player?

Decide the key roles that will be instrumental in seeing this game to successful fruition. Be sure to represent the "thesis" within the list of roles. For example, if you take the family firm, ensure that your family is accorded a role, i.e. as recipient of the extra money that you are requesting. In the example of the "mercenary firm," research and quote the most senior executive who has been an advocate of the "reward" principle.

Thesis / Roles / **Aim** \ Power-principle \ Pay-off

What is the overall purpose of the game?

The "aim" of the game is in fact the means to the end; the "end" or "pay-off" in this instance being getting more money. You do this by setting up a series of transactions between you and the decision makers which will be viewed as helping push the corporate agenda (not your own!) but which will also yield a pay-rise for you. This might seem a far-fetched or tortuous way of getting a pay-rise. But the management very often has to justify (or legitimize) its actions in granting you a pay-rise. This legitimization brings power into the frame. Better for you to define the power game than somebody else – for it might result in a different endpoint.

Certainly, your own past performance will be a critical factor in assessing your pay-rise. But the future is more important than the past – for it is the future performance that holds the key to success of all the decision makers. This can be leveraged by appealing to corporate beliefs, such as the family, which are there to guide the firm to success.

Thesis / Roles / Aim / **Power-principle** \ Pay-off

Which is the dominant principle: belief or fear?

Work out which will be the dominant one in driving the game forward. In the "family company" you should use the belief principle, for you are invoking a shared value to which the whole company can or ought to be able to subscribe. You are loyally restating a core corporate credo and using it to leverage the management towards giving you extra money.

In the "mercenary" environment, it is probably better to use the fear principle. This could be articulated as: if the company does not stick to its stated practice of rewarding success, then it risks (hence fear) losing not only good staff but also direction.

Thesis / Roles / Aim / Power-principle / **Pay-off**

What are the ulterior motives?

Be clear about how much you require and how often you will need to be remunerated. If your gambit is taken up strongly by the management – then go for more – you get what you negotiate.

The pay-rise game: sample template

Thesis
What does the game seem to be about?
Helping you make a better home for your family.

Roles
What is the role of each player?
Identify the full list of decision makers and work out their likely input into this game. Your role is as "home-maker"; also your family will have a role as recipients of the extra money.

Aim
What is the overall purpose of the game?
Use the pay-rise as an opportunity for the company to re-state visibly its commitment to the family.

Power-principle
Which is the dominant principle: belief or fear?
Belief.

Pay-off
What are the ulterior motives?
More money.

The getting promoted game

| **Thesis** | Roles | Aim | Power-principle | Pay-off |

What does the game seem to be about?

Getting promoted can often (but not always) go hand-in-hand with getting a pay-rise. However, getting promoted is more explicitly a power-game in the sense that the pay-off is extra power. Your first step is to identify a "gap" in the corporate armory and choose a thesis that addresses it. For example, "innovation" might be both a key corporate value and also an area of current deficiency for the organization. Get associated with it – the solution not the problem! This will provide a good set-up for the game.

Thesis / **Roles** \ Aim \ Power-principle \ Pay-off

What is the role of each player?
Again, the full set of decision makers will need to be identified; assign yourself the part of the "innovation maker" in the process, or even proposing a task-force to address the issue. Identify any influential advocates of innovation within the organization and attempt to form some type of relation with them. Recruit them as ambassadors for you in the promotion process.

Thesis / Roles / **Aim** \ Power-principle \ Pay-off

What is the overall purpose of the game?
The aim of the game should mask the selfish act of you accruing more power for yourself. Rather, in the example of "innovation" above, the aim could be articulated as "let's get innovation back to the heart of our organization" (with your promotion of course a vital part of achieving this).

Thesis / Roles / Aim / **Power-principle** \ Pay-off

Which is the dominant principle: belief or fear?
Try "fear," i.e. that the organization is losing its edge – it needs to get back on track or risk (hence fear) failure. Also use some belief, i.e. in you being one of the agents of change for the better.

Thesis / Roles / Aim / Power-principle / **Pay-off**

What are the ulterior motives?
Be clear about how much promotion you require to suit your ambition – it be might be granted to you incrementally. If so, agree each stage and objectively benchmark each success. By the way, don't get associated with a project that is doomed to failure. Power means not just responsi-

bility for making sure that something happens, but also the authority to drive it through.

The getting promoted game: sample template

Thesis
What does the game seem to be about?
Innovation.

Roles
What is the role of each player?
Identify the full list of decision makers and work out their likely input into this game – especially influential innovation ambassadors; your role is as "change-maker."

Aim
What is the overall purpose of the game?
Getting innovatory behavior back into the organization.

Power-principle
Which is the dominant principle: belief or fear?
Fear; belief: fear that the organization is losing its edge; belief that you can help change things for the better.

Pay-off
What are the ulterior motives?
More power – promotion.

POWER GAMES
AND THE
CORPORATION

Making Power

THE LEADERSHIP GAME

- ◆ The leader doesn't need to know more – you just have to believe (or fear) that he does
- ◆ The leader is always a little distant from his followers – it is that distance which allows him to govern – remember the space between the light and the cells in the Power Doughnut? That space was a necessary part of the apparatus so that it could work effectively.

The scene

Being a sector or department head or director puts you on a new footing. But it also places you onto a level playing field with other department heads/directors – a level playing field in the sense that each is considered equal. Of course, there will always be corporate bias depending on the culture, with accounting or marketing or R&D carrying a greater or lesser command on the resources. As the Stanford academic Jeffrey Pfeffer points out,

"We have already noted the way to gain power is not only to obtain control of a resource, but also to make the resources that one controls more important."[1]

It is, therefore, this next step (making the resources that one controls seem more important than other sets of resources) that the power relations really ratchet up.

But this still does not cover the question of the "will to power." Why does one quest for power in the first place – or indeed do we all really crave it in the same way?

Polling of executives coming through London Business School on executive training consistently shows that "power" is the biggest motivation for executive activity.

The interpretation of this (during these candid and off-the-record conversations) seems to be that it is power on its own basis, for its own sake, which drives the executive forward.

Not merely power to achieve things. What is interesting is that it is power *on its own* basis that is the goal: the self-conscious "savoring" of the activity of wielding power itself. In this regard, power is like some drug that has been released from its utilitarian functions and used "recreationally," i.e. to savor its own effects.

The attraction of leadership: tasting pure power

There can be little doubt that many desire power for its own sake rather than just the trappings. Political life is traditionally more poorly paid than the private sector. *However*, the thought of being the most powerful person in the state/county/country is clearly attractive to many. Indeed, it is seen to be a laudable aim to have one's eye on "higher" office. And let us please, at this juncture of the book, see the aims of such office, *viz.* "to do some good for society," "to make a difference," "to implement one's vision," for what they are: acts which in themselves invoke legitimation in order to attain/maintain a position of power.

It would seem that the possibility or the likelihood that many seek power just in order to savor its effects has ethical implications.

This is because ethics and ethical people have most difficulty with pursuits that are self-referential. To seek pleasure for its own sake is considered hedonistic. To seek happiness for its own sake is selfish. Quite often traditional "ethical" teachings would claim that happiness comes through forsaking personal interest and dedicating activities to some other end.

The search for power, the desire to savor it on its own basis, is a "potent" and seductive experience. The corporation is one of the few areas left in contemporary society in which the individual can (acceptably) experience what it is to wield power over others.

As American statesman and man of letters Alexander Hamilton noted: "In the main it will be found that power over a man's support (compensation) is a power over his will."

But to savor power on its own basis is not necessarily immoral. The challenge is to differentiate between "good" and "bad" uses of power in an organization. Of course, without power, everything would grind to a halt.

Leaders of tomorrow

New thinking about the role of the leader in tomorrow's corporation would claim that the *donut* model (of control and compliance) is outdated and the hallmark of a dinosaur organization. London Business School/Harvard academics Ghoshal/Bartlett argue that stifling the creative and entrepreneurial spirit of the corporation makes for an organization incapable of meeting the challenges of tomorrow. A new "moral contract" between company and employee is called for:

> *"Companies operating under this new contract must strive to create a new and invigorating work climate ..."*[2]

They cite many examples of corporate systems of organization that seek to enlighten rather than constrain the employee. This is clearly evident through examples such as ABB and 3M, which have changed the rules of the corporate game. The question for us here, though, is: have they changed the rules of the power game – or are we just seeing different "theses," while the aim remains control and compliance?

Philosophically, this is a business-take on the liberal humanist tradition. This tradition would be most horrified by the power donut way of locking an individual into the fixed spatial relationship with the corporate body.

It is fair to say that there are many organizations around which are led by leaders who instil fear throughout. But what if we were to contend that the Ghoshal/Bartlett take on business culture (or indeed in the De Geus model of the "Living Company") simply involves giving priority to the belief principle in the power equation and deprioritizing the fear principle.

In other words, the executive is "inspired" by the dominant corporate mission and thus is feeling motivated, mobilized and oriented towards helping the corporate mission. The scenarios examined earlier (e.g. the corporation versus the employees) indicate that *belief* is often a more productive *power-principle* than fear. But the model of the living company, or the inspired and entrepreneurial workforce, does not necessarily mean we are out of the power game. Have we merely not adapted the initial gambit to local or contemporary conditions? If this is so, then the inspired worker is no more free than the executive working in a regime of fear. He may feel a whole lot better about his lot. He may like giving back more to the company. His company may receive increased commercial benefit as a result of this extra drive. But nevertheless he is still in the power donut. The cell bars may be made out of gold, and the supervisors' light a relaxing ambient, but no serious qualitative difference exists.

I remember a senior executive of a major healthcare firm saying to me: "this is not a particularly nice place to work. If you want to feel love then spend more time with your family. This is, however, an exciting place to work – which is why I stay."

The new *leadership charter* calls for empowering the individual, creating an internal entrepreneurial culture or inspiring team-based innovative behavior; for breaking industry rules so as to generate and maintain a competitive edge.

All of these factors (and more), which would seem to be key to keeping ones corporate health, are still all rooted in the primary power-play as examined in this book. It isn't just about the corporate leadership becoming more sophisticated, thereby masking more successfully the real (dominating) intent of management. That is too simplistic a take on what we are experiencing.

We have (as explained using the Berne rubric) an increasingly sophisticated way of playing the same old power game. Framed like this, we have ever more elaborate (Machiavellian) "theses" in modern business.

Anecdotally, this would mean that the corporations that are successful in the near future will need to invest more effort and resource into its initial gambits (e.g. stakeholder value; employee value; environmental commitments; good neighbourhood values) and so forth. We see this around us so much that it seems natural (as opposed to a ruse in a game) that an organization would want to have these concerns. Taking care for the environment above and beyond regulatory mandates would be an example. In another 150 years, who is to say what an organization will care about? Certainly 150 years ago, care for the environment was not top of the agenda.

Somewhat contentiously, I would argue that the new trends or moves towards a "liberated" type of corporate leadership are in fact no more than different moves within the same old power game, which (as we have seen) has compliance/control at its heart.

A new move in the leadership game is identified by White *et al.* as a move toward uncertainty:

> *"Leaders are usually seen as creators of certainty ...*
> *"Walsh's (and others) philosophy is that CEOs must deliberately place themselves in a position of uncertainty by showing vulnerability ... They must demonstrate that they don't know all the answers ..."*[3]

It might *feel* better for the employee under the regime of the "vulnerable leader" – but that is as far as it goes. It might also be a more commercially expedient way for the leader to play the game. But feeling free doesn't mean you are necessarily out of jail.

The chainsaw versus the corporate democrat

The 1990s have seen two approaches to leadership with differing results that might point to a commercial *modus operandi* of the future: those of Al "Chainsaw" Dunlap and Jonathan Ledecky.

The *Fortune* article of June 8, 1998, the magazine claims, was the first to herald the fall from grace of Dunlap as head of Sunbeam:

> *"Dunlap, a remorseless cost cutter and bottom-line man, is finding life at the top of the food chain a scary place. After the meeting with analysts, where he announced 5,100 layoffs, the stock fell almost 2 points. It is now hovering around $25, off more than 50% from its high in March. Ironically, it may be Dunlap's mania for maximizing shareholder value that finally does him in."[4]*

An article in Barrons points to the tough "unpeople focused" approach of Dunlap:

> *"Dunlap shocked the multitude at Crown-Zellerbach, then Lily-Tulip, then Scott Paper and most recently Sunbeam. He closed plants, fired workers by the thousands and executives by the hundreds, abandoned product lines by the dozens.*
> *"Then he committed public literature. He bragged in his book that he was happy and proud of actions that caused pain for so many others. In the goopy wishful-thinking world of the 'nineties, that made him 'mean-spirited.' "[5]*

Perhaps the fall of Dunlap presents itself as the symbolic decline of the pure shareholder-driven philosophy and an implicit acknowledgement that people can also matter in an organization – not just the financial data. Indeed it is a false distinction between the two. This certainly is the case for Jonathan Ledecky, who by his late 30s had presided over a number of billion-dollar corporations with his stock holdings conservatively estimated at $200 million.

The highly personable Ledecky is the instigator of what he terms "corporate democracy":

> *"It's a very big part of my philosophy of operating. It expects that if you treat people like partners and colleagues instead of*

like employees, you're going to end up with a much better re-sult."⁶

On one side the Chainsaw, unabashed about the huge human cost of restructuring a business. On the other, a new type of leader who has restructured the office products business and is now engaged in a similar venture with the facilities management business. He has made many of the employees joint-owners through stock options. All without the savage bloodletting visible at Sunbeam. Again, though, are we not seeing just the two basic power principles of the power game in action: fear (the chainsaw) and belief (corporate democracy)?

Ledecky on power⁷

Question: If you give more "power" to your employees, does that not mean ultimately you have less yourself and will therefore have to share owner value more democratically. All fine if the pie is growing but perhaps not so if it static or shrinking

Answer: *No, you end up increasing the empowerment of your people who actually give you more power as a result because their respect level for the leader goes up. They come to realize that the corporation is adopting their input. As for ownership, the very fact that they have become owners through stock options makes them better corporate citizens and cuts waste. I liken it to the difference between the way you treat a rental property you might be renting versus a home that you buy. I don't think the pie shrinking or growing really makes a difference here.*

Question: Is *corporate democracy* just another more enlightened way of binding the employees into higher productivity and therefore just another rhetoric equal in value to the chainsaw rhetoric?

Answer: *No, it has nothing to do with productivity, although that certainly is a positive by-product. More to do with the philosophy of leaving in place the managers and employees of the acquired entity rather than replacing them or eliminating them in the name of productivity.*

Question: Do you see real changes in manager-employee relations whereby there is a more democratic sharing of power and if so does this not lead to slower and more unwieldy decision making processes or fragmented responses to competitive challenges?

Answer: *No, actually decisions get implemented faster once ownership of the decisions has been translated to the field ... in other words, since we tend to listen to field based feedback, the affirmation of the feedback by corporate enables the field to go forward with confidence.*

The particularly interesting aspect of the first answer lies in the phrase "increasing the empowerment of your people who actually give you more power as a result because their respect level for the leader goes up." Surely equivalent to the internalising of the power relations within the power donut? There the inmate/worker has (through the belief power-principle) ended up governing himself (equal to the autonomy of "empowerment" for Ledecky). The inmate/worker has also ended up reciprocating and increasing the power of the supervisor/owner through this transaction ("your people who actually give you more power as a result").

Here "corporate democracy," while being a handy tag-line to fuse a corporate and political humanism is also a way in which owner value can be safeguarded, a prime (if not solo) motive of business.

The game

| **Thesis** | Roles | Aim | Power-principle | Pay-off |

What does the game seem to be about?

Creating certainty and charting a plan for the organization.

As White *et al.* point out,[8] the role of the leader has been to give a sense of purpose, some certainty, to the organization. Even if the leader under a new charter has to demonstrate vulnerability or uncertainty, he still moves the organization forward by asking the questions, sharing his unease with some of the corporate assumptions. In this way, certainty will be brought closer to the grasp of the organization as a result of the endeavor of the leader.

Thesis / **Roles** \ Aim \ Power-principle \ Pay-off \

What is the role of each player?

There are a number of roles that the leader himself can adopt in getting the job done:

1   *The Coach:* facilitator and mentor to the organization; based on the sporting model, this leader has been and done most things already and offers technical expertise along with experience (Robert P. Goizueta, former head of Coca-Cola).

2   *The Dictator:* heavily directive style and based on a military model, this leader (like Henry Ford) seeks to instruct not only the objective of the organization, but the way in which those objectives are achieved (August Bush – Anheuser-Busch).

3   *The Explorer:* seeing the future and describing it back to the organization: through corporate visions, missions and so forth, the explorer seeks to mobilize his team to follow him into the new land he sees (Bill Gates, Microsoft).

4   *The Provocateur:* like Socrates of old, this leader does not offer easy solutions, but continues to provoke the organization into questioning its orthodoxy – closest to the White model of offering vulnerability (Percy Barnevik, ABB).

5   *The Parent:* commanding respect (faith and fear) from the organization, this type of leader is primarily concerned with encouraging higher and reasoned rules of corporate performance and behavior (Sam Walton, Wal-Mart).

6   *The Prince:* based on Machiavelli's character, this leader may be a great "pretender and dissembler" – this leader will stop at little to achieve his ends, ruling by the most pragmatic and expedient means possible (Robert Maxwell, Mirror Group).

7   *The Bridge:* apparently a weak leader and the other management seem to walk over him – but also like the bridge, he can get them to the other side (John Major, ex-Prime Minister, UK).

8   *The Great Man:* born to be a leader; commanding respect automatically – is plugged into the future and what it might hold for the organization (Thomas Watson Sr, IBM).

Thesis / **Roles** / **Aim** \ **Power-principle** \ **Pay-off**

What is the overall purpose of the game?

Maintain an information imbalance between you (the leader) and the rest of the organization.

That is what is key to the leader being in and maintaining a position of power. The leader knows more necessary relevant information than the rest of his management team – for that is his value.

Even if the leader is displaying vulnerability or uncertainty, implicitly he is saying: "I do not have all the answers, but you have even fewer." The leader will have a vision of the future that the organization may mot be privy to. Or perhaps he has a sense of organizational or marketplace perspective that the organization cannot achieve. Perhaps the leader has a historical view that gives a breadth of experience craved by the organization. And so forth.

Thesis / **Roles** / **Aim** / **Power-principle** \ **Pay-off**

Which is the dominant principle: belief or fear?

The power-principles vary according to the role the leader adopts:

1   *The Coach:* belief in the fact that he knows more than you do; faith in his skills
2   *The Dictator:* fear – do it or you are out
3   *The Explorer:* belief, in that you believe he knows where the organization is going or needs to go; fear of the unknown – the explorer gives certainly in the face of the vast unknown
4   *The Provocateur:* belief in the superior wisdom of the leader
5   *The Parent:* belief in their status within the organization; fear of retribution or parental disappointment if not successful
6   *The Prince:* fear – if you cross this type of leader, who knows what might happen to you – or when
7   *The Bridge:* belief, if not in the individual himself, at least in the role of and the need for a leader
8   *The Great Man:* belief: in the Great Man's ability to get the organization to where it needs to be.

| Thesis | Roles | Aim | Power-principle | **Pay-off** |

What are the ulterior motives?

Why an ulterior motive? The thesis revolves around the altruistic act of providing some shape for the organization to grow and prosper. The pay-off of leadership is selfish and lies in the personal pleasure experienced through exercising power over another. Granted, there is a professional pride in seeing one's decisions come to fruition. But how often have we seen leaders – either commercial or political – cling to a position of power even when doing so clearly damages the organization or position that they apparently cherish?

Summary of the leadership game

Thesis
What does the game seem to be about?
Providing shape and certainty to the organization.

Roles
What is the role of each player?
1 The Coach
2 The Dictator
3 The Explorer
4 The Provocateur
5 The Parent
6 The Prince
7 The Bridge
8 The Great Man.

Aim
What is the overall purpose of the game?
Create and maintain an information imbalance between the leader and the organization.

Power- Principle
Which is the dominant principle: belief or fear?
Belief; fear – depending on the role.

Pay-off
What are the ulterior motives?
Personal pleasure experienced from the exercise of power over another.

The discussion

"What was that theory – mushroom management – keeping the people in the dark – fill them with bullshit? Is your leadership game not just an elaborate version of that?" I asked.

"It is not about lying to your organization," said Niccolo. "Implicit in the definition of a leader is the ability to inspire either belief or fear (or both) in the employee base. Do not forget your power donut. Without power, the leader ceases to be. From the chainsaw through to the corporate democracy of Ledecky, both these principles are apparent and both are key to the leader functioning properly.

"Yes but how do you get to be a leader?" I replied. "What you are saying is perhaps relevant for the leader to maintain or consolidate his position. How do you get to be behind the light in the power donut?"

Niccolo replied: "We have already covered much of this in the power games concerning the individual – from maintaining power over subordinates, i.e. through the strategic manipulation of the space they occupy (call-centre game), through to the getting promoted game, which should set you on your path to leadership."

Niccolo continued: "becoming a leader is perhaps one of the most selfish tasks you can set yourself. It calls for the ability to impose your will and systems on another – in the belief that your way is somehow better than another's.

"Of course, you do not necessarily need to be more accomplished than another – you just need to convince others of that, so that you can be invested with the power of a leader."

"But I cannot help thinking this is a very cynical take on leadership," I replied. "Surely the leader can be a force for good in the organization – while you are framing it as a purely selfish act?"

"The leader can be a force for great good or for destruction within the organization," replied Niccolo. That is a fact. However, how a leader gets to that position, how the leader maintains and grows the strength of his position of leadership – these were the questions we were pursuing, I believed."

"Well, yes ..." I replied. "But ...

"And do you doubt that the logical, ruthless and selfish pursuit of power – in inspiring belief and fear in others – will yield the required ends – that of becoming a leader?" prompted Niccolo.

"It probably will ..." I conceded. "I just thought there were, well, nicer ways of getting there."

Niccolo chuckled. "You can moderate the tone of the power game, by adjusting the tone of the 'thesis.' However, be in no doubt, young man, that it is a game which is played very seriously, although few have the stomach to play it well."

Notes

1   See Pfeffer.
2   S. Ghoshal and C. Bartlett, *The Individualised Corporation* (New York: HarperCollins, 1997).
3   R,White, P. Hodgson and S. Crainer, "Seekers and scalers: role models for future leaders," *Training & Development*, January 1997.
4   P. Sellers, "Exit for Chainsaw?" *Fortune*, June 8, 1998.
5   T. Donlan, *Barron's*, June 22, 1998.
6   C. Murphy, "Cutting-edge Strategist," *Franchising World*, March/April 1998.
7   In conversation.
8   See White *et al*.

Breaking Power

THE ACTIVIST GAME

The scene

The battle between the corporation and the activists groups is a power struggle of epic proportions, which can damage each side. It is a battle for scientific fact; a battle for the hearts and minds of we the general public. In short, it is a battle for the truth!

The struggle between the corporation and the activist is a complex and involved one. Let us take, therefore, a recent classic: the struggle between Shell and Greenpeace over the dumping at sea of the Brent Spar. To do so we must "set the scene" by reprising in detail the chain of events that led to one of the world's most powerful companies being brought to its knees. The struggle between Greenpeace and Shell is also going to be important in understanding the media game.

Brent Spar: the battle between Royal Dutch Shell and Greenpeace

A year after the conflict over the dumping at sea of the Brent Spar,[1] Shell declared that:

> *"Brent Spar is no longer just a North Sea installation, but a unique and defining event. The challenge now is to ensure that*

it defines a new stage in the regulation of business which en-
joys the hearts as well as minds."²

But what exactly was being defined? What had happened to one of the world's biggest corporations when it conceded that an oil rig – a simple tool of the oil trade – was being used as a tool to change the regulatory conditions of its business?

The centre of balance had moved away from the business – it had lost control over how it wished to conduct its own affairs – and it had done nothing illegal! The way it wished to conduct its business was being partly handed over to those who knew little and cared even less about the oil trade.

Having taken the Brent Spar out of operation, Shell, the world's biggest petrol retailer, surveyed a number of options to dispose of the facility before deciding to dump it in the north Atlantic. The disposal plan was approved by the UK Government in February 1995, which also informed the other EC member states. However, on June 20 1995, just four months later, Shell postponed its plans to dispose of the Spar at high financial and corporate cost to itself and embarked on a wide public consultation process.

The aborted disposal mission was expected to cost in the region of $14 million. Two years later at the Shell's annual general meeting, a number of shareholders filed a resolution asking for named board members to be responsible for environmental affairs as well as calling for external review and audit procedures to be instituted.

Nevertheless, both Shell and the UK Government maintained that dumping the Spar at sea remained the Best Practicable Environmental Option (BPEO).

So what happened?

First, let us look at the history behind Greenpeace's attempt to get into the business of lobbying against oil companies.

Although Greenpeace had attempted to protect US coastal waters by campaigning against oil drilling/prospecting in ecologically sensitive areas as far back as 1983, it was not until 1989 – after the Exxon *Valdez* sank in the Prince William Sound, Alaska, spilling 40 million gallons of oil – that Greenpeace formally began to campaign on oil. Greenpeace acknowledged the difficulty of such a campaign because of the Western world's obvious dependence on oil.

This made for a more complex campaign message to be pushed out – as distinct from saving baby seals, for example – which was always a simple and effective fund-raising platform.

Greenpeace set itself two targets with respect to the oil campaign:

1   to highlight "dubious" industry practices; and
2   to attempt to educate the public on alternative sources of energy.

A series of oil disasters in the next few years began to give opportunities for Greenpeace to push out their message:

· pollution linked to oil wells in Siberia in 1991
· in 1992, the *Haven* caught fire and sank in the Mediterranean
· in 1993 the *Braer* oil tanker ran aground off the coast of the Shetland Isles, part of the UK, releasing twice as much oil as the *Valdez*.

Of course, the difficulty for Greenpeace lay in the fact that it could not actually try and block the normal progress of oil tankers around the world; that would have resulted in the loss of some public support.

Additionally, when an oil disaster struck, what could Greenpeace usefully say aside from "we told you so." It could perhaps help in the clean-up activities, as when it lent the rescue services an oil boom when the oil tanker *Rose Bay* ran aground off the coast of Devon in the UK. No sexy headlines there.

The Greenpeace formula

The key to Greenpeace success lies in the emotive "action" shots of activists in boats getting sprayed by water cannon as they attempted to stop some activity or other. By personifying moments of conflict, Greenpeace has always been able to deliver to its membership and beyond vivid images that capture the essence of the opposing positions. The problem with oil spills is that, while there can be many and varied victims such as wildlife struggling in the oil, it is harder to single out the culprit. Of course, the offending ship, which is leaking this oil into the sea, is certainly the cause. But too often it can also look the victim as it lies helpless on some rocks, or veers aimlessly on the tides. The real issue facing Greenpeace – up until the Brent Spar incident – was how to package the issue *with their role specifically spelled out*. Feeding grotesque and upsetting pictures out to the hungry media coupled with environmental warnings and prescriptions was simply not enough. The static and moving pictures must also demonstrate Greenpeace doing its job: saving the world.

The opportunity ...

Half-way through 1994, Greenpeace became aware that the UK Government was reviewing plans for disposing obsolete rigs at sea. Greenpeace was later to claim that its only interest at the time was to present its arguments against sea dumping. Regardless of whether that was ever really the case, in December of 1994 the UK Government's Department of Trade and Industry wrote a key report. This was in favor of the disposal at sea of the Brent Spar. The path was laid open for what was to become one of Greenpeace's most successful campaigns.

Part of Shell's problems throughout the affair could be summed up by Cor Herkstroter, chairman of Royal Dutch (the Dutch half of Royal Dutch/Shell), as "technical arrogance." In other words, once the technical aspects of the problems had been investigated and a decision taken, an arrogance and lack of sensitivity to the other side of the issue would set in. As far as Shell was concerned, it had done its bit by commissioning the leading offshore engineering and marine contracting firm McDermott. They had reached the conclusion that the sea disposal of the Brent Spar constituted "deep sea disposal."

This was then proposed to the UK Government, which was happy to issue a licence. Anything else, as far as Shell was concerned, was secondary.

The technical bases had been covered and there was little need for the organization to concern itself with a debate on the subject. Moreover, it considered (mistakenly) that just because it had the law on its side, it could just force the issue through.

The Bay of Rigs

The battle on the Brent Spar, which in Shell's own words was to become a "unique and defining event," was planned by Greenpeace in March of

1995. Their gameplan: to place a number of activists on board. Greenpeace knew that Shell had only a limited amount of time to dispose of the rig before the inclement weather of the North Sea began to set in after the short summer. Their mission: to delay the disposal operation as long as possible in the hope that the "window of opportunity" would pass.

On April 30 four activists clambered on board and raised the banner – "Save the North Sea." The victim had been identified and this time Greenpeace was on hand in a visible and eminently communicable fashion. The message to their membership and beyond: this time we can stop an oil disaster before it actually happens ...

Greenpeace's media apparatus captured these "defining" moments and broadcast them to news agencies across the world.

Greenpeace was later to recall that the atmosphere once aboard was eerie:

> *"In the office areas there was still a great deal of information in the cupboards and personal effects such as postcards – it's as if everybody left in a hurry. The movement of the sea made loose doors creak open and shut, adding to the illusion of the ghost ship."*[3]

After two weeks of occupation, the first sign of erosion in Shell's comfort zone had occurred. Up until this point, the fact that the UK Government had granted a licence had at least limited the argument from a regulatory perspective. However, on May 12 1995, the Danish Government criticized the granting of the licences. The regulatory sweater that was keeping Shell warm was beginning to unravel. Later that day Shell served a legal eviction order on the protesters.

Shell attained an interdict from a Scottish court stopping the resupply of the Spar. An attempt by Greenpeace to relieve the protesters on board on day 17 of the occupation was aggressively hampered by Shell.

Further unravelling of the regulatory position continued when Germany, Belgium and Iceland joined the protest against the granting of the licence. The UK Government stood firm. Things then began to move very quickly indeed.

Countdown to corporate failure

- *May 18:* Shell gets an eviction order naming Jon Castle – the Greenpeace leader on the Spar.
- *May 24:* An oil rig support vessel, several times the size of the Brent Spar arrives on the scene and police and security finally manage to remove the protesters.
- *June 7:* Greenpeace manages to place more protesters on the rig and hang a banner – "Save our Seas." They are driven off by water cannon.
- *June 9:* Ireland joins the protest against the granting of a licence.

Over the next 10 days ...

- Mounting pressure on the UK Government from other country representatives continues. Again, the UK Government stands resolute.
- Media attention on the issue escalates.
- Greenpeace organises protests at Shell offices across Europe.
- Public protests at Shell service stations across Europe including gunfire aimed at a service station in Germany.
- *June 20:* Greenpeace manages to place two activists on board the Spar. Shell backs down on the plans to sink the Spar. The Brent Spar is dragged away by the defeated tugs and a huge rainbow (Greenpeace's logo) is visible in the victorious sky

An unexpected turn: Greenpeace apologizes

In September, Greenpeace apologized to Shell because it had actually miscalculated (and overestimated) the amount of toxic waste that was on board the Spar. The amount of toxic waste on board had played a key part in Greenpeace's argument that the Spar should not be dumped at sea. In a release, and public letter of apology, Peter Melchett, executive director of Greenpeace stated:

> *"The argument was about whether it was right to dump industrial waste of any sort in the deep oceans, whether dumping the Brent Spar would be a precedent for dumping other oil installations, and indeed other wastes in the oceans, and, fundamentally, over whether we should dump wastes into any*

part of the environment, as opposed to reducing waste, and recycling, treating or containing harmful materials.

"Our view remains that the division between us on the Brent Spar depends on how deeply we value our environment, and what damage and precedents we find unacceptable. As information about our sampling on the Brent Spar was made available to the press, I am making this letter similarly available, and I would be grateful if you could convey my apologies to your colleagues on the Board of Shell UK."[4]

Later that month, the two sides moved closer together when Greenpeace publicly welcomed 21 out of the 29 proposals being considered by Shell for the disposal of the Spar. Greenpeace commented:

"The signs are that Shell is now following the logic of environmental responsibility and public opinion."[5]

The net result

Shell's power over one of its own vessels, with a full and legal disposal licence, had been taken away from it by a group of protesters acting illegally and with inaccurate data about how much waste was on board in the first place.

Although Shell's share price seemed to have been largely unaffected by the saga, it does admit that the debacle over the Spar may have cost them "a great deal" in the short term. There is a host of oil rigs waiting to be disposed but the rest of the oil industry still appears afraid to go down the same road as Shell – each wants the other to go first; as Greenpeace smugly remarked, "there is a race to come second."

The game

"While you rapturously pose as deriving the canon of law from nature, you want something quite the reverse of that, you strange actors and self-deceivers."

Nietzsche, *Beyond Good and Evil*

- ◆ Will activists ever be satisfied?
- ◆ Should you pursue an "open and honest" dialog with activists?
- ◆ Is it in the interests of activists to resolve all concerns quietly and out of the public eye?

Thesis \ Roles \ Aim \ Power-principle \ Pay-off

What does the game seem to be about?

The thesis of the activist game is set up as:

Activist: "I care more about the environment than you do. In fact, you seem to want to destroy it. We, therefore have to try and protect it as best we can, although we do not have the resources you do ..."

Corporation: "That's not fair. We also care about the environment, but there are other considerations also."

In other words, the thesis is set up as a simple opposition between environmental care and environmental destruction.

The "love-child" in this tug of war is of course the environment. Or should we say the Environment. Because it is not just about the seas and lands around us. It is the Environment as an "absolute." Which is to say, that here the Environment assumes the same exalted status as justice or freedom. These are unarguable values that underpin that way we operate. We do not question them or those who we accept as their agents.

Of course, the principles of freedom and justice and so forth are radically political. I say this because as soon as they enter the equation, they bring with them the question of power. Who is on the side of freedom and justice? Who is against them? How shall we protect these things that we hold sacred? These are issues that call power into play.

In the same way, those who align themselves with the Environment similarly place themselves in an absolute (invulnerable) position: "Mess with us and you mess with our Environment – and you don't want to do that do you."

The key question to be asked here is *how* did Greenpeace manage to thwart Shell so utterly over what was in fact a fairly simple operation? Not just by means of slick media manipulation and a few well-timed excursions onto the platform of the rig. They managed such a deep success by luring Shell wholly into a brand of the activist game.

In the letter of apology to Shell, Executive Director of Greenpeace, Melchett summed up the parameters of the "thesis" as we have explored it:

> *"Our view remains that the division between us on the Brent Spar depends on how deeply we value our environment."*

The Environment itself is the fundamental organizing principle of the thesis. The Environment is the unquestionable absolute that Melchett claims Greenpeace cares more about, is closer to, is more protective of than Shell. Empirically, this may or may not be the case, but as we saw, scientific or empirical data has actually little to do with the rules of this game.

The clever initial maneuvers in this activist game were:

1   Greenpeace establishes the position closest to the Environment.
2   Greenpeace sets out its stall – and establishes a distance between itself and Shell.
3   This necessarily places Shell further away from the Environment.
4   This in turn makes it a lot easier to expose Shell's motives (profit/ greed) and not Greenpeace's. Why not the latter? Simply because of its proximity to the Environment.

5   From the beginning of the game Greenpeace is at an advantage, although it *seems* to be the more helpless.

Whether Greenpeace is actually sincere in its motives with regard to protecting the environment is actually (and perhaps surprisingly) irrelevant. This is because the issue of "saving our sea" allows Greenpeace to engage in what is a sophisticated and almost invisible form of power play. As Nietzsche claimed in *The Will to Power*, "every drive is tyrannical." Now, of course, most will not share such a view. But in this game, let us at least admit that the link with an unarguable absolute such as the Environment is always and everywhere politically interested – and therefore implicated in a power-play.

The other huge strategic advantage for Greenpeace in its proximity to the Environment is this issue of invisibility. As we saw, we are not inclined to question Greenpeace's motives because of its close alignment with the Environment.

In other words its motives are nigh on invisible. Invisible "power-plays" are of a higher calibre than power plays that we can see. A case in point: take Western governments' hold over the population as opposed to that of developing world governments. We know that the latter need visible and violent forms of coercion more frequently in order to maintain a hold on power. This is actually because their grip on power is weak. Western-style democracies need to use police baton-charges on its civilians much more rarely. This is not just because these civilians are naturally more peaceable. It is because the power relations that govern us all in the developed world are more mature and sophisticated than elsewhere. Frankly, there is rarely any need for violence. We have internalized most of the power relations and govern ourselves for the most part.

Shell allowed Greenpeace to set the agenda and thereby was always one move behind. For example, it was only when Shell's public policy position began to crumble (May 12 – Danish Government criticizes the granting of a licence) that it served the eviction notice on the protesters. It is probably fair to assume that Shell had been seeking to hold off as long as possible from tactically engaging with Greenpeace on the Spar. Scuffles at sea with corporations or law enforcement representatives is the sea activist's forte – so that the latter move would have been to the delight of Greenpeace.

Finally, another key advantage accorded Greenpeace in this formulation of the activist game also extends from its alliance with the Environment. This has to do with scale.

We shall see in the next game that the media very often casts its stories in terms of biblical/quasi-biblical narratives – e.g. *Search for the Holy Grail* and *David versus Goliath* (in which the underdog wins over the greater force).

We have seen that the Greenpeace alliance with the Environment has permitted it to engage in a covert power play which places it in a strategically stronger position than its opponent.

It is also now able to draw out the opponent onto the Spar – and cosmetically invert the relations. In other words, at a hidden level Greenpeace is in the stronger, more powerful position than its opponent, *but* it then consolidates this superiority by making itself appear (to the outside world) as the weaker player. It does this by casting itself in the David versus Goliath role (i.e. pre-packaged for media distribution) and luring Shell into a display of force.

Shell again plays into this trap by sending along the vast oil support vessel the *Stadive* (several times larger than the Spar itself) in order to evict the protesters. By resorting to asserting its physical dominance, Shell implicitly acknowledges its inferior position in the activist game. In some ways, the resort to physical assertion is a last resort – there were no better cards left to play. Moreover, the huge scale of the *Stadive* plays into the hands of Greenpeace's David versus Goliath set-up. The *Stadive* encapsulates the corporate "Goliath" versus the Greenpeace "David." Shell unwittingly provides Greenpeace and the media with this narrative about which the world knows two things: who is in the right (David, played by Greenpeace); and what is the outcome (David wins). As academics Winter and Steger comment in their book *Managing Outside Pressure* in the section discussing the "activist check-list,"

> *"If Shell had used this checklist, it might have foreseen that its platform was an ideal target for Greenpeace and that Greenpeace stood a good chance of coming out as the victor of the campaign."[6]*

| Thesis | **Roles** | Aim | Power-principle | Pay-off |

What is the role of each player?

This is a complex game with many parties, some of whom are playing more than one role. For the purposes of analysis and clarity, let us keep to the main protagonists. This game is essentially a four-hander, split into two camps.

1 and 2   Greenpeace and the media
3 and 4   Shell and the UK Government.

1   Greenpeace – environmental guardian angel

We have already examined the tactics engaged in by Greenpeace in some detail. The part they play in this whole saga is, of course, the protector of the environment. In case anybody is ever in any doubt, the "save our seas" placards sum that position up. The space they occupy in the public psyche is very complex and too involved to examine here. Suffice to say that they are taking on a role that would traditionally have been associated with government-appointed regulatory bodies.

The very existence (let alone the phenomenal success) of the activist groups is generally an indictment of the government–public trust axis. Greenpeace and its ilk can only have gained success in a gap created by the erosion of public trust in government who, it seems, can no longer be completely trusted to get on with its job.

The advancement of the secular society (religious institutions losing status), the advent of scientific relativism (Godel's Incompleteness theorem) and so forth can all be cited as things that may have prompted such a breakdown in trust.

The space created by this breakdown is a privileged one, however: for it is a location associated with nothing less than truth, of *certainty that it is so*. The breakdown in public trust has allowed the shrewd activist group to don the mantle of the old high priests – whose traditional roles were to act as conduits to the people of these higher truths.

Ironically, some religions, having suffered the humiliating marginalization of the secular society, are now using environmental activist tactics to gain back some of the lost territory:

"In 1995, leading members of nine major religions met to dis-
cuss the environment both in Japan and at Windsor castle in
Britain (where the host was Prince Philip, president of the World
Wide Fund for nature).

"In 1996, in San Francisco, various religions pondered a
'Charter of Human Responsibilities,' a document promoting
care of the planet and various other wholesome ideas."[7]

2 Media – environmental collaborator

The media and the activist group form a mutually supportive relationship – both feeding each other. If the activist group is the seer of truths
hidden to us mere mortals as we go about our daily lives, the media is
the mouthpiece. What use is it having thirteen activists aboard the
Brent Spar if the media does not run with it. In fact, some half-dozen
journalists actually boarded the Spar along with the activists – there to
record the scenes of conflict and feed the images through to the waiting
world.

The media, of course, does not actually need to share in any of the
beliefs of the average environmentalist. The rapport is based on a deep
mutual understanding of the real needs of the other and the media is
happy to be knowingly used like this. When the media does not play
ball, of course Greenpeace is not slow to retaliate. The BBC produced a
series entitled *Scare Stories* with which Greenpeace took issue:

Richard North of the BBC comments:

> *"When Greenpeace said the dumping of Brent Spar in the North-*
> *east Atlantic was obviously wrong, I rang every marine scien-*
> *tist I could think of and most of them said that it really wasn't*
> *likely to be much of a problem or indeed any sort of a problem*
> *at all. And they were quite robust about it."[8]*

In the long and vitriolic response issued by Greenpeace bemoaning bias,
please note the reference to a "licence" which in view of the whole licence
saga for the dumping of the Spar is actually quite funny:

> *"Greenpeace regrets the fact that the BBC, which now has no*
> *serious Current Affairs coverage of the environment, failed to*

use the opportunity of this expensively made series to create a
genuine and open debate on the very important issue of why
we should protect the world on moral and ethical grounds,
and what role science can and cannot play in telling us what is
right or wrong ...

"*Despite its often repeated criticisms of Greenpeace for sup-*
plying video footage, for this series the BBC also used Green-
peace footage without obtaining a licence to do so. This is bad
practice and may have been unlawful."[9]

3   Shell – behemoth culprit

If Greenpeace has produced a victim (or potential victim) out of the
North Sea, then Shell fulfils the role of nasty culprit. Being the world's
largest petrol retailer is good pedigree for the profile of culprit. Being a
giant multinational oil processor, Shell is already at a disadvantage in
the public mind when it comes to environmental issues.

As we have seen, Shell played its role beautifully in defining the problem during the attempted disposal of the Brent Spar in purely technical
(what is the most expedient means of disposal?) and public policy (the
UK Government will grant a licence and not revoke it) terms. In both of
those categories they were correct (strictly speaking) and this would
have been sufficient in most scenarios.

However, in this instance, Greenpeace managed to change the rules
of the game, a game in which the technical validity of Shell's case as
well as the "legitimacy" of their intended actions were both down-val-
ued.

4   UK Government – corporate ally

Just as the media proved to be such a valued collaborator to the Greenpeace activists, so the UK Government proved itself a valued if flawed
ally in the Brent Spar issue. In fact, their steadfastness in the face of
other countries beginning to bridle may have given Shell a false sense of
security and bolstered their "technical arrogance." Just as the media
legitimated the actions of Greenpeace by reporting them, so also the UK
Government carried out a similar role in legitimating the proposed actions of Shell. Unfortunately for this camp, it was not to be enough.

| Thesis | Roles | **Aim** | Power-principle | Pay-off |

What is the overall purpose of the game?

The aim of this game was for Greenpeace to gain a position of power from which to launch future oil environmental campaigns. As we saw earlier, at the beginning of the 1990s it was difficult for it to gain a foothold, given the nature of the problem. They could not be seen to be saviors once the oil disaster had happened and it would have been publicly unacceptable for Greenpeace to hinder the journey of oil tankers.

| Thesis | Roles | Aim | **Power-principle** | Pay-off |

Which is the dominant principle: belief or fear?

Belief (in the Environment; akin to the unquestionable religious faith). A little fear there as well: Behind the overall subscription to the Environment lies the fear of world disaster should we not choose to kneel at this particular altar.

| Thesis | Roles | Aim | Power-principle | **Pay-off** |

What are the ulterior motives?

For Shell, the aim of the Brent Spar game was to establish its credentials in the area of oil rigs, and use that position to negotiate with the oil companies over their future activities. The pay-off has been to gain a central position of power within the oil debate. Remember the game was supposed (thesis) to be just about care for the environment. If negotiated cleverly (and there is no evidence to suggest otherwise) Greenpeace would be able to bargain with the oil barons and use its control over the disposal issue to leverage its opinion on other areas of operation.

Remember, there are over 75 large deepwater platforms operated by Amoco and Unocal, among others, which are due for decommissioning and which could legally qualify for sea disposal.

After the Brent Spar episode, it is hard to see how Greenpeace would not be one of the most significant power-base each oil company would have to deal with in planning these disposals. Less than 10 years after the Exxon *Valdez* oil spill, Greenpeace had maneuvered itself into a prime bargaining position.

In the last chapters, we came across the issue of the ulterior motive as that which both defined the game as such and which differentiated the game from merely a set of manoeuvres. Greenpeace never said that what it wanted was a position of power. All it apparently wanted was to make its arguments known to the UK Government:

> *"Ironically in the light of what happened later, at the time the only planned Greenpeace response to this review was to lobby the interested parties and present a report with the organis-ation's arguments against sea dumping."*[10]

Today it is Greenpeace who needs to be lobbied on the future of dumping at sea. Does this sound like an accident to you? Clearly the pay-off is the fact that Greenpeace has established its own position of power at the centre of the oil debate. From there, all it needed was to retain that grip on power.

Summary of the activist game

Thesis

What does the game seem to be about?
Environmental protection versus environmental destruction.

Roles

What is the role of each player?
1 Greenpeace – savior of the environment
2 Media – ally to the activists
3 Shell – corporate behemoth
4 UK Government – ally to the corporation.

Aim

What is the overall purpose of the game?
Greenpeace, the central figure in the issue of deep sea disposal of oil rigs maintains and increases membership.

Power-principle

Which is the dominant principle: belief or fear?
Belief; fear.

Pay-off

What are the ulterior motives?
Greenpeace undermines the power of the world's largest petrol retailer – and gains power for itself.

The discussion

Niccolo smiled. "It is not very nice is it – to stride so gracefully and yet to have to stoop so low."

"I do not understand why it all got so out of hand, I replied." "Surely at the end of the day, the law of the land has to prevail and people will have to abide by it – regardless of whether they feel it is right or not."

"Certainly" replied Niccolo; "but when you rebut like with like – where does that leave you? The UK Government's position was called into question by other regulatory powers. While that may not have been enough in this instance to shift the UK Government's position, it did go a long way in neutralizing the public impact of that decision. You see, people need to believe in some absolutes and when the other governments began to question the granting of the licence, considerable strength was lost by Shell."

"But why? – the UK Government was still going to hold strong."

"Because the main weapon in Shell's armory had been considerably blunted. Because other countries began questioning the right of the licence, inspired directly or indirectly by Greenpeace, and this was enough to refute a considerable part of Shell's gambit. Again, if you remember, it was just when the Danish Government raised an objection to the licence that Shell began to engage tactically with Greenpeace. At this point they were losing ground all the time."

"OK," I replied, "I understand how the loss of power occurred in this instance – but what else could they have done? They had done their homework (which Greenpeace clearly hadn't). They had submitted to the relevant authorities and it had been accepted. What more should they have been doing?"

"In theoretical terms," said Niccolo, "they should have sought to unmask the thesis of the game. They should have sought to engage in what we might term the 'anti-thesis'. For it is only by undermining the factors that hold the thesis together, that Shell could have hoped to win the battle.

"You need to address the direct core of Greenpeace's proposition," he continued, "that is, its relationship with the environment. The tasks, and they are by no means easy ones, are:

"*Firstly, expose Greenpeace's care for the environment as not disinterested – the environment is only a pawn in its quest for power.*

"*Secondly, expose Greenpeace care for the North Sea as an arbitrary (the opposite to truth) selection in its overall drive for a position of power with reference to the oil companies – this would reposition Greenpeace as just opportunists rather than a group with genuine care for the seas per se.*

"*Thirdly, achieve a higher ground in the public and public policy eye on the environment, thereby corrupting Greenpeace's privileged position.*

"*Fourthly, seek to substitute a different first principle – in place of the environment – public need for fuel to keep civilization on track, for example.*

"*Perhaps, fifthly, establish an alliance with a different (more moderate) activist group – which will innoculate the organization against further attack.*

"*None of this would have been easy to do and without the benefit of hindsight, perhaps it would have been difficult to make the argument internally to allocate the resources to achieving these ends.*"

Niccolo continued. "*While I am no expert on the oil business – and it is some time since I have been involved in the business of lobbying Government – it seems to me that Shell could have attempted to bolster the UK Government's position by encouraging other Governments to come out in support of the licence – after all it seems in this case that the science was fairly strong. Shell is the biggest petrol retailer in the world, after all, and oil is a resource that all countries depend on heavily. Could it not have used its considerable market strength invisibly to advance stronger Governmental support rather than visibly using its might against a handful of protesters in the full view of the public?*"

"*But could they not have talked with Greenpeace – explained the science to them and come to some type of conclusion?*" I replied. "*Perhaps, that way, all of this unpleasantness could have been averted.*"

"*Indeed – but that is to misunderstand the real nature of the interaction,*" corrected Niccolo. "*It is only by means of the loss of power by Shell and its ilk that Greenpeace can grow stronger, increase its membership, and so forth. To come to a happy resolution on issues such as this would be to deny the very core of Greenpeace's being. It exists to combat on issues. Without combat – without visible moments of con-flict – it would cease to be what it is.*

"Viewed thus, and I am trying to be realistic about the nature of power, rather than cynical about the nature of activist groups," said Niccolo. "It is not in their interests to resolve all of its issues quietly – for that is the role of government."

Niccolo concluded: "Of course the corporation can seek to engage in discussions with the activist group, but of course not to share privi-leged information, for that would be to weaken its own position. Nei-ther merely to seek a quiet resolution, for that would be to weaken the activist's position. There are a number of advantages to having discus-sions: perhaps to demonstrate that you have attempted to resolve the issue, to say that you have engaged openly and meaningfully – this might be of advantage down the line. Similarly, perhaps you could offer the activist another issue upon which it can protest – which might do you less harm but with which they might be equally content, and perhaps even enjoy your tacit support.

"But let us move on," said Niccolo.

"Let us move on to another external opponent who is a constant threat to corporate power – the media."

THE MEDIA GAME

The scene

"Television is not the truth – television is a goddamn amuse-ment park."

Network

Howard Beale, the character in the 1975 film *Network*, was getting to the core realization about the nature not only of TV but of the media generally. Peter Finch played the lead role of an aging TV anchorman for UBS, who has been fired but who still had two weeks to go. Under extreme pressure he begins to turn into a TV prophet/lunatic making grand pronouncements about the media, society and the interplay between the two. In a supreme act of cynicism, which is also a moment of astute media performance he declares:

"I would like at this moment to announce that I will be retiring from this program in two weeks time because of poor ratings. Since this show is the only thing I had going for me in my life, I've decided to kill myself. I'm going to blow my brains out right on this program a week from today. So tune in next Tuesday. That should give the public relations people a week to promote the show. You ought to get a hell of a rating out of that. Fifty share, easy."

In the last chapter we saw that the proximity between the activist group position and the absolute Environment was a power-play; a strategic move that established a dominant role in the power relations with Shell. Shell accepted this set-up and then failed to gain control of the game.

We also witnessed the symbiotic relationship between Greenpeace and the media – both understanding what the other needed to thrive. Both fed each with the raw material and also with the "cover" necessary to win the game. Clearly this was a successful partnership as it mobilized public and Government support for a review of the licence to dump the Spar at sea.

The Media Charter

In the US there is a history of journalism as a venerated profession linked closely with the right of "freedom of speech." Walter Cronkite, ex-CBS anchorman, was for many years the most trusted man in America. In the UK, journalism is much less venerated and instead there is a history of media ownership, making overt bias much more acceptable.

Brill's Content, the US magazine that monitors the media, divides its charter (and by implication, the rest of the media's charter) as:

- accuracy – stories should be true
- labeling and sourcing – information should be clear and unnamed sources labeled as such
- conflicts of interest – content should be free of any motive "other than informing its consumers"
- accountability – journalists should "hold themselves as accountable as any of the subjects they write about."[11]

CNN president Ted Johnson, speaking to a major conference of editors, publishers and media executives, posed the media challenge as:

> *"meet[ing] the changing expectations of their readers and viewers with innovative and creative approaches while maintaining accuracy and fairness."*[12]

This view contains the same assertion that Howard Beale made at the top of the chapter (TV not being about the truth but instead being an "amusement park"). In other words, while the media has as its holy grail "accuracy and fairness," the reality is that it needs to entertain and amuse the consumer or go out of business.

The "innovative" and "creative" paths indicated by Johnson above do not only apply to the ways of reporting but to what is being reported (i.e. not just to the packaging of the message but to the message itself). Summed up by journalists, it is the challenge between "truth" and commercial intent, as if there is an automatic distance between the two – between "good journalism" and the "bottom line."

If that is what the more sophisticated elements of the media struggle with on these away days and naval gazing expeditions, these tensions, as we shall see, also pose the threat as well as the solution to the power struggle between the corporation and the media.

For in the same way that the activist group regularly profits at the corporation's expense, so too does the media.

Accurate and fair?

Just after the bombing in Atlanta's Centennial Olympic Park, Robert Jewell, a former law enforcement officer, had his first taste of the public life.

Initially it was positive: Jewell was hailed as hero when he reported the back-pack (which turned out to contain three pipe bombs) to the Georgia Bureau of Investigation in July of 1996. Jewell was interviewed on CNN and NBC.

However, soon afterwards, Jewell himself became a suspect in the bombing. This heralded a media feeding frenzy. Despite the fact that there were no formal charges against Jewell and indeed no real evidence, the broadcast media began to take the role of public investigators. As one reviewer noted:

> *"Tom Brokaw, the anchor of NBC Nightly News, reported on the day that suspicions about Jewell were publicly revealed that his arrest was imminent. An Atlanta TV station even showed the barber shop where Jewell got a haircut prior to an interview with Brokaw. At one point, at least one network broadcast live from outside Jewell's apartment 'as if a hostage drama were unfolding.' At another point, even the sight of Jewell's frightened dog being led across the lawn was 'deemed sufficiently fascinating to make the nightly news.'"*

In October, the District court judge, prior to forcing an end to Jewell's ordeal (who was never charged), compared the media coverage to an "Italian movie that portrayed reporters as vultures."

Clearly, the media industry is undergoing considerable fragmentation due to the onset of online, cable, satellite and digital modes of delivery. This leads to cut-throat competition for viewers, listeners or readers, which increases the pace of the hunt for a good story.

But what we see in the case of Jewell is not really that different in kind to the way the media has always operated. It is not a case of commercial pressures forcing the otherwise worthy journalist into situations ever more tacky and tawdry in an attempt to survive transition to the 21st century.

The media claims to have "accuracy and fairness" as its compass. It also claims the public interest (right to know) as its mandate and freedom of speech (democracy) as its legitimation. But there is an altogether more fundamental principle at work: simply that the media needs to maintain the interest of the reader. It is that straightforward: know your reader and survive; ignore and die. It is also that complex because the reader and his values and tastes are constantly changing.

Jimmy Breslin, the hallowed New York-based journalist, sums up the core media imperative when he says: "the biggest felony a journalist can commit is to be boring."

Truth out! Interest in!

Of course many journalists would argue that to deviate from the truth is the biggest felony. You see, invoking the "accuracy and fairness" automatically casts the journalist as both the seeker of truth (on the side of good) and also the interpreter of truth (even better) on behalf of the public.

However, what if we accept that the real opposition underlying the role of the journalist is like an axis with "interest" at one pole and "boredom" at the other.

This would place the *National Enquirer* (US) and *The Sport* (UK), for example, at the end that puts a priority on reader entertainment.

At the other end of the axis we have the "quality" publications: the *New York Times* (US) or the *Sunday Times* (UK). Is there really any substantial difference between the two poles – apart from the fact that one has increased the entertainment element in the customer offering?

This may seem an outrageous assertion – who would want *The Na-*

tional Enquirer or *The Sunday Sport* to be the guardian of our democracy and our right to freedom of speech? However, it could also be argued that these papers operate almost exclusively in offering us what we want (sleaze, fantasy and the incredible) rather than what they think we need, and are therefore more sensitive and accurate barometers of the public mores and tastes?

The media and distance

Before looking at the relationship between the corporation and the media, it is worth spending a little time looking at the issue of "distance" – distance in the simple sense of the gap or space between the media and the subject being reported. This drives to the heart of the "accuracy" principle cited by Johnson at the top of the chapter. It is loosely equivalent to "objectivity" (i.e. truth) as opposed to "subjectivity" (i.e. opinion). The premise I am introducing works as follows: for the media to feel it is doing its job, to feel comfortable and centered in its functioning, there must be an element of distance. In short, the journalist needs to maintain a proper "distance" between himself and the subject he is writing about in order to do his job properly.

We shall see later in the game that one of the secrets to gaining power back from the media lies in closing down this distance between the media and its subject.

This will allow the corporation to get off the defensive, a situation that so many executives feel is inevitable when it comes to media handling.

The death of Princess Diana and the loss of media distance
A prime example of the loss of distance in a social/cultural context happened in August of 1997, when Diana, Princess of Wales, died in a car crash in Paris.

Firstly, this was a big, big media event with many offshoots to keep the story going (engagement to Dodie; role of the paparazzi; her possible pregnancy; murder theories). Her death represented the loss to the world of a great public figure.

At the same moment, it represented the birth of an enduring global icon and brand (valued at over $200 million one year later). The difficulty for the media during the first week of blanket coverage was that it was itself part of the story; it had no distance.

A handful of photographers at the scene of the crash were arrested on suspicion of actually causing the crash, or at least with not providing sufficient help at the scene (an offence under French law). Instead they were accused of taking pictures of the dead and the dying. Many papers were also regular purchasers of the photographs taken by these paparazzi.

The media challenge

The media had to focus on its *own* role in the story while also reporting the story itself. The overall media discomfort was apparent throughout the first few weeks of the affair. This was particularly apparent during the funeral service when Diana's brother turned his vitriol on the press (many editors were present).

This attack on the media received applause from the tens of thousands lining the streets outside. This loss of distance made it all the more difficult for the media to cover the story properly.

It resolved this dilemma by creating a false distinction and thereby some measure of distance. But how?

The paparazzi were disowned by the rest of the journalists. They were shunned as not being part of the same industry at all, but merely social pariahs. This shunning was not just prompted by revulsion over the so-called actions of the paparazzi. It was also the means by which the media could achieve this distance and enable proper coverage.

The corporation from the media perspective

The traditional (and usual) relationship between the successful multinational corporation and the media is one of distance. This suits the media.

There is also a fair measure of mutual distrust. This makes the corporation feel defensive, careful and generally unforthcoming.[13]

From the media perspective, the multinational appears to be quite often closed. The corporation is perceived to engage in activities that suit only its own agenda (rather than the public interest).

Additionally, many corporations are thought by the media to have an unfair influence on public policy and its access to decision-makers through its ability to hire teams of high-priced lawyers, lobbyists and spin-doctors.

The media from the corporate perspective

From the corporate perspective, the media can often be seen as a voracious consumer of reputations. For them, the media is an entity with blind disregard for the facts and ignorance of the industry issues facing the business. In the view of many executives with whom I have spoken about the subject, there is a general consensus that the media for its part has an unfair influence on the marketplace and customers. One properly timed negative story can affect share-price, trade relations and customer loyalty all in one go.

From a corporate perspective, such a stance and set of beliefs only reinforces the power relations between the inside and outside of the organization. Distance is maintained and this will generally suit the media. In power terms, this is why the media seems to be at an automatic advantage over the corporation.

When I asked a chief executive (who was facing a corporate catastrophe) what was the worse thing that could happen from then on, he replied: "I could lose my job." So the media can have an impact on personal and professional status, as well as the executive's income. This does not make for an atmosphere in which the corporation can easily overturn the media game.

At a corporate level, many organizations have close relationships with the press through the levels of their advertising spend, which can often work in their favor.

The game

- ◆ Is the media more interested (generally) in entertaining or informing its readership? If both, which has primacy?
- ◆ How do you give the media what they want while safeguarding your reputation?
- ◆ Can the media be trusted?

Thesis \ Roles \ Aim \ Power-principle \ Pay-off

What does the game seem to be about?

In the last chapter, the thesis of the activist game was set up between environmental care and environmental destruction. Essentially (as this game was constructed) big business was set, if not antagonistic to then at least distinct from the needs of the Environment.

This was also (fortunately for Greenpeace and unfortunately for Shell) a power-play – a classic means of leveraging and maintaining a position of power. We also saw that the proximity to the Environment (or any other such absolutes) both masked and simultaneously increased the power relations.

Masked in the sense that the pursuit of an absolute (such the Environment or Justice or Truth) is an unquestionable, altruistic and worthy act in itself. This deters anybody from unmasking the real motives. *Increase* in the sense that the proximity to the absolute as we have seen gains a power advantage.

The thesis of the media game is essentially the same. One just substitutes "Truth" for the *Environment* in the last game. The Environment and Truth are both cited by the respective parties (activists and media) as the overall motivators.

This equivalency also allows the media and the activists to work together so closely. On the Brent Spar, we saw that a number of journalists actually installed themselves on the structure along with Greenpeace representatives. Greenpeace successfully closed down the distance between itself and the media allowing for easy media manipulation. This is an interesting case in point when discussing media "distance." To manipulate the media you just have to look for a means to close down that distance.

The fact that the media was on board the oil platform certainly allowed reporting on the story as it actually happened. But how could "accuracy and fairness" be maintained in such an arrangement?

The thesis of the media game could be articulated as:

Media: We are the seekers of what really is going on – it is our job to hold you to account. Our readers have a right to know.

Corporation: Yes of course the readers have a right to know, but we have a right to stay in business and provide our shareholders and our employees with proper value. The truth is all very well but there are commercial realities that must also be borne in mind.

Thesis	**Roles**	Aim	Power-principle	Pay-off

What is the role of each player?

These roles can be taken as breaking out into three broad (quasi-biblical) categories:

1   David versus Goliath – the fight of the "little guy" versus the giant
2   Wise King Solomon who decides between the forces of good and evil
3   the Quest for the Holy Grail.

1   David versus Goliath

The David versus Goliath narrative is much favored by the media because it is easy to portray and can be very visual. There is clearly strong public appetite in reading/viewing about the "small guy against the big faceless corporation." The Brent Spar is a good example, where David (Greenpeace) takes on the mighty Goliath (Shell). We see it time and again, and the stronger or more visible it is the more it fits the bill of Goliath. And as we saw with the case of the Brent Spar, the dice are loaded against the corporate perspective. This role is also much favored by the activist groups: it is easy and ready-made for public consumption.

Similarly, the media likes to take on some of these mantles: David versus Goliath (the media on the side of the weak – protecting them against the cruel forces of the mighty). The fact that some of the most powerful corporations on earth (determined by their capability to influence opinion and therefore to make things happen) are media monoliths (Murdoch; Turner) is an irony which seems to be partly lost.

2   Wise King Solomon

This is a variation of the David versus Goliath situation – David was on the side of good. Here the media, rather than just being on the side of the "little guy," sees it as its mission to reveal and therefore battle the injustice all around. Corporate injustices against employees, customers and the environment all make for a steady diet of exposés. The media in this role is on the side of the good (i.e. the truth) cutting through corporate dissembling and delivering "accurate and fair" comment.

3   The Quest for the Holy Grail

Classically, this is the investigative reporter who knows that there is a story (truth) out there. It just needs to be unearthed. Sometimes the corporation can be the one hiding that story and therefore becomes one of the hurdles that must be overcome in this quest. The reporter becomes an intrepid knight, the seeker of the Holy Grail. The corporate world becomes the land of the dark and evil forest which must be penetrated by the knight.

In summary

The role of the media, therefore, shifts between the roles outlined above depending on what is being reported. The generic stance remains one of "third party," independent, objective body of representatives (4th Estate) that sorts out the truth and other values society holds dear.

| Thesis | Roles | **Aim** | Power-principle | Pay-off |

What is the overall purpose of the game?

The aim of the media is in its own terms to maintain and increase readership. It does this by processing, packaging and distributing information to the taste of its audience. This is in fact no different a process than any other business transaction involving consumers. Without this ability to tailor and sell the information to its audience, the media product loses its support base and will perish.

| Thesis | Roles | Aim | **Power-principle** | Pay-off |

Which is the dominant principle: belief or fear?

Belief; that is, belief in "truth" – which is the currency used by the journalist. If the media power-base is threatened – as in the case of the UK press in the aftermath of the death of Diana, then the media will resort to "fear": "If you let our power by dissipated through regulation, then the individual's right to freedom of speech is also diminished – and hence the democratic process."

| Thesis | Roles | Aim | Power-principle | **Pay-off** |

What are the ulterior motives?

The classic stand-off between the corporation and the investigative journalists looks like this: On one side we have the nasty big business which possesses secrets affecting many lives, jobs and perhaps even the environment, in which we live. The corporate need is to keep controversy to a minimum (stock markets don't like it) and continue to focus on owner value. On the other hand there is the media, suspicious as ever. It tries to trip up the executive, get him/her to say things he/she doesn't want to in order to steal a march on its media rivals and increase audience.

In reality, the media merely uses this "truth" (it claims to hold so dear) as raw material in order to produce interesting fodder for audiences to consume. Within that key contract lies the real intent of the transaction. The media is able to use the information achieved from the enclosed organization to snag and hold the audience attention (that which interests) and can therefore achieve the following:

- commercial (increased advertising revenue);
- social (ability to lead and even shape perceptions on issues of public value);
- political (ability to swing voters); marginalize the "extremists."

Summary of the media game

Thesis

What does the game seemd to be about?
Truth versus corporate dissembling.

Roles

What is the role of each player?
1 David versus Goliath – the fight of the "little guy"
2 Wise King Solomon – who judges between good and evil
3 The Quest for the Holy Grail.

Aim

What is the overall purpose of the game?
Maintain and increase readership.

Power-principle

Which is the dominant principle: belief or fear?
Belief; fear.

Pay-off

What are the ulterior motives?
Commercial, social and political power.

The discussion

Turning to Niccolo, I said: "I find all this rather shocking. Yes there are always regrettable aspects of any industry but to categorize the media as purveyors of mental chewing-gum is surely to do them and their entire readership a profound disservice?"

"I am not that interested in describing and concluding on what the media is – for it is not one homogenous entity, but varies in kind and in strength from territory to territory" Niccolo replied.

"Rather, as pertinent to our conversation here about the efficient functioning of power, we should focus our interest more properly on how the media functions and here you can see much similarity across disparate territories. It is during this exercise that we can see more clearly that the media is a reflection of, allied to and ultimately supportive of the apparatus of state."

I interrupted: "But you cannot say that. Everywhere we see examples of the media holding the government to account on its election promises, criticizing them when they lie to the people. To paint them with the same brush as the agent of propaganda in a totalitarian regime is ludicrous."

Niccolo could see how agitated I was becoming and moderated his voice to a more gentle, considerate tone. "Look, we started this conversation with a view to exploring power and how that power could be harnessed and refined within the corporate structure.

"We have sought to explore how the individual can get ahead more quickly utilizing this knowledge for his own or his company's benefit.

"Getting too deep into a political discussion will veer us too far off-course. Let us agree that the media is bound up in a complex and sometimes paradoxical set of relations with the society in which it operates – both leading and following public opinion at the same time?"

I nodded.

"And let us agree that without the support of its readership – that organ of the media will cease to exist – or at least cease to have any further meaningful role to play."

I nodded again.

"*Good,*" *said Niccolo. "Then let us assume that if the corporation is to defend against or even beat the media, it needs to understand intimately how the relationship between the media and its audience works?*"

"*So what you are implying,*" *I interjected, "is that the leveraging of the audience does not necessarily have to be at the expense of the corporation?*"

"*Exactly*" *replied Niccolo, smiling once again.*

"*We are back to our last conversation about the activist group?*" *I asked.*

"*In many ways yes,*" *said Niccolo, "and in some ways the media and the activists are inseparable. Certainly they can travel parallel journeys. But while the corporation has to engage in a direct struggle with the activists, it has to work* **through** *the media. Beating the media will never mean putting it out of business because the corporation also needs the media to communicate its commercial affairs with its audiences.*"

"*Are you saying that the corporation should lie to the media for its own ends – because, if what you say is right, truth has gone out the window?*" *I asked.*

"*The difficulty with lying these days,*" *sighed Niccolo is that it can so easily come back to you in ways that are undeniable.*"

I had to laugh.

Oblivious, Niccolo continued. "If the media is not in fact working on a truth versus lie structure (our thesis), then it might be a profitable exercise to adopt a similar posture to see if it can be exploited."

"*You are losing me again,*" *I warned.*

"*My point is,*" *said Niccolo, "that perhaps the media is not really a purveyor of truth to its audiences. Perhaps it is in reality engaging in a commercial enterprise that shapes raw material and then distributes this product to its consumers. This would make the media enterprise little different from most other commercial enterprises. There is no reason, therefore, why the corporation under pressure from the media should really be under a different type of pressure than it would normally be when, say, under threat from a competitor.*"

"*But that is not going to change the fact that the media can report damaging facts about the company and relay that to millions of people instantaneously. Any amount of theorizing is not going to change that fact," I replied.*

In a slightly exasperated tone, Niccolo continued: *"But that is to play the media game and to lose it, probably." To see them as pursuers of truth is to lose sight of how the corporation can actually gain the upper hand."*

"Well, go on – how can they then?" I challenged.

"To see the media as mere pursuers of the truth is to place the corporation into a static role. This role is as defenders of the corporate values under threat from outside forces. It needs to protect certain information from the outside gaze. That automatically places the corporation in a retrenched, defensive position.

It makes the corporation less willing to engage the opposition actively, not willing to form strategic alliances with the opposition wherever necessary. So the first concern to be addressed is what you moderns might term 'mind-set'. In any battlefield it is hard to win when your preoccupation is not to lose!"

"Granted," I interjected.

"Additionally, defending a fixed point, both literally and figuratively, is rarely an advantageous position unless naturally well protected. Better to pick the scene of battle as far from your front lawn as possible. For if one loses the first skirmish, one has precious little territory left to retreat to, in order to bolster the troops."

"Yes but we are not talking old-fashioned battle here?" I questioned.

"True, so let us then require the corporation to adopt a more dynamic model than the one we have just mentioned. Let us say to them: 'Be bold, take risks, be assertive; pre-empt strikes; do the things you would normally do when stalking the competition.' In some ways the media can be more lethal than the competition because they can appear to have nothing to lose.

"This is not so: they can lose readership, they can lose advertising revenue; they can lose access to future 'interesting' information about your industry, which your corporation might be able to control and so forth.

"As in any gameplan, you just need to work out where the pressure points are and apply."

"You mentioned a more 'dynamic' model earlier. What did you really mean by that?" I asked.

"In some ways the media operates a 'guerrilla warfare' approach: short, opportunistic sorties into your territory to attempt to gain some quick, minor victory."

"You are back to your battlefields again," I sighed.

"All right," said Niccolo. "The modern corporation could consider applying the 'advocacy' model which it uses in the court of law more widely and particularly with the media. This means," said Niccolo, noticing my bemused expression, "that the corporation should concern itself less with what information it will disseminate and which it will seek to retain and more with making a 'case' to suit a specific local position. In other words (before you ask), the corporation should not lie. It should in fact cast off the usual truth–falsity polarity. It should replace it with the legal one: that which is valid and that which is invalid. For in the modern justice system, truth is negotiated.

"This in fact is more in keeping with the nature of the struggle – an indirect external one. As in the court of law – the opposing barrister is not actually the one who needs to be convinced. It is the jury. In the same way, in the struggle with the media for the 'truth' – it is ultimately the audience of each medium that must be convinced, not the journalist himself. He is not an endpoint himself merely a 'medium.' "

Out goes truth and falsity; in comes valid and invalid

"The corporation should instead seek to offer a position to the media and validate it with verifiable facts. This position can change from moment to moment and will always be sustainable so long as they are supportive facts. That, in short is a dynamic model and one that will aid the corporation if it desires to combat the 'guerrillas' in a more effective fashion."

I interrupted: "And you can offer particular aspects of the media particular positions that you know will be of more interest to their readers and favor some over others – leveraging their own competitiveness.

"Then, through forming these alliances, you can close down the media distance, making it harder for it to strike at you in the same way that Greenpeace struck up a deal with the media on the Brent Spar?"

"Now you are getting the measure of it!" replied Niccolo.

I continued: "And if the corporation is rigorous in its planning, it will ensure that the series of current and future positions will not invalidate each other, for that would be counter-productive."

I looked disconsolately out of the cabin window at the ethereal clouds as the sunshine caught them before the sun set.

"It is all so very ..."

"Machiavellian?" offered Niccolo.

Notes

1　Constructed in Norway in 1976, the Brent Spar had seen some fifteen years of service in the Shell/Esso Brent Field in the northern North Sea – the UK's largest source of gas and oil. Shell compared the Brent Spar to an "iceberg" with most of the bulk lying beneath the waves. The Brent Spar weighed in at 14,500 tonnes with the huge tanks displacing 66,500 tonnes of water. Its prime job had been as a giant floating oil storage and loading buoy storing oil from the Brent "A" platform, as well as acting as a tanker loading facility for the whole Brent oil field.

2　http://www.shellexpro.brentspar.com/

3　http://greenpeace.org/

4　*Ibid.*

5　*Ibid.*

6　M. Hunter and U. Steger, *Managing Outside Pressure: Strategies for Preventing Corporate Disasters* (Chichester: John Wiley & Sons, 1998).

7　"Thou shalt not covet the Earth," *The Economist*, December 21, 1996.

8　http://greenpeace.org/

9　*Ibid.*

10　*Ibid.*

11　Masthead, *Brill's Content.*

12 Quoted in "Good journalism and bottom line," July 19, 1997.

13 This and much of the next section is based on workshops in which I have participated; These workshops were devised by Paul Gillions, International Managing Director, Burson-Marsteller.

Games You Can Play

The market dominance game A

> ◆ In a finite marketplace, the relation between you and the corporation is always about "power?"
> ◆ If your competitor is citing high-minded principles (e.g. fair competition) – is this a ruse in a power-game? How so?

This first game is to be played from the perspective of an organization that does *not* enjoy market dominance. The game should be played in order to gain some market share from the dominant competitor. Game B outlines an approach that contains some suggested counter-moves by the dominant competitor.

Thesis	Roles	Aim	Power-principle	Pay-off

What does the game seem to be about?

Identify a "thesis" or key value which will set the game up. We need some absolute that will be able to sustain the game. Fairness might work. Remember Netscape *et al.* versus Microsoft. It just doesn't seem "fair" that one company has such a market presence; it is counter-intuitive.

Thesis / **Roles** \ Aim \ Power-principle \ Pay-off

What is the role of each player?

The thesis will then determine the types of roles you adopt. For example, if you go with "fairness" – then you automatically need both a *champion* for "fair play"; a *culprit* – one who is being "unfair; a *victim* – one who is suffering from the act of unfairness.

Pick a victim other than yourself. Rather, position yourself as the champion of market fairness. The victim might in fact be the customer – because too much competition can imply lack of customer choice.

Thesis / Roles / **Aim** \ Power-principle \ Pay-off

What is the overall purpose of the game?

The "aim" of the game is in fact the means to the end; the "end" or "pay-off" in this instance being getting some market share for yourself. The aim of the game will be to force a change in market trading conditions that will be more conducive to your own business. In the Netscape example, it would mean that Microsoft would have to include some option for *Windows* customers to use the Netscape browser.

Thesis / Roles / Aim / **Power-principle** \ Pay-off

Which is the dominant principle: belief or fear?

Work out which will be the dominant one in driving the game forward. If the thesis is "fairness" then it is best to use the "fear" principle. It could be articulated thus: "if there is a market correction then there will be a risk (hence fear) to the way business normally operates – with companies going out of business, a decline in consumer choice, lack of innovation in the sector and so forth."

Thesis	Roles	Aim	Power-principle	**Pay-off**

What are the ulterior motives?

Be clear about how much market share is required so that you can benchmark the success of the game.

Summary of game A

Thesis

What does the game seem to be about?
Fairness versus unfairness.

Roles

What is the role of each player?
1 Victim (customer; small business; Innovation)
2 Culprit (competitor)
3 Change-maker (regulator)
4 Champion (you).

Aim

What is the overall purpose of the game?
Change trading conditions so that they are more conducive to your business.

Power-principle

Which is the dominant principle: belief or fear?
Fear.

Pay-off

What are the ulterior motives?
Get some market share off your competitor.

The market dominance game B

This next game is to be played from the perspective of the organization that enjoys market dominance but who is under threat (e.g. from a regulator) with regard to that dominant position. The game should be played in order to chart out some counter-moves.

Thesis \ Roles \ Aim \ Power-principle \ Pay-off

What does the game seem to be about?

You need to come up with a thesis that will directly address the initial game as presented to you. For example, in Game A, the gambit concerned the issue of "fairness," which masked the competitor's intent of gaining some market-share from you. I suggest in this instance that you come up with a thesis that will address one of their "victims," e.g. customer choice. Doing so will allow you to address the emotional subject of diminishing customer choice and keep you out of a mere rebuttal situation. In other words, merely to prove that your behavior is in fact "fair" is to accept the game as set out by your competitor – not a good idea if you remember Shell. If you can address the issue of customer choice successfully, you will be able to neutralize the impact of one of their most powerful moves.

Thesis / Roles \ Aim \ Power-principle \ Pay-off

What is the role of each player?

The roles will follow the thesis. Your role will be as "champion of consumer choice." Of course you will need tactical examples to validate this! If possible form an alliance with the regulator, given that they are also about protecting consumer choice. If possible, move their role to one of "patient parent" – presiding over squabbling children but not wanting to take a particular side – *this will make direct action by them less likely.*

| Thesis | Roles | **Aim** | Power-principle | Pay-off |

What is the overall purpose of the game?

The aim clearly is to prevent any change in trading conditions – and to allow you to do business unhindered.

| Thesis | Roles | Aim | **Power-principle** | Pay-off |

Which is the dominant principle: belief or fear?

Ironically, you can chose the same power-principle and for the same reasons as your competitor. You can argue that your market presence guarantees customer choice and stimulates innovatory behavior. And also that if the market starts getting over-regulated, then there is a risk (hence fear) of the consumer missing out in the long term.

| Thesis | Roles | Aim | Power-principle | **Pay-off** |

What are the ulterior motives?

Your pay-off will be continued regulatory and consumer permission to do business in the fashion you have done so up until now.

Summary of Game B

Thesis
What does the game seem to be about?
Consumer choice.

Roles
What is the role of each player?
1 Champion of consumer choice (you)
2 Patient parent (regulator)
3 Competitor – self-serving; and causing confusion in the consumer by spurious arguments.

Aim
What is the overall purpose of the game?
Maintain trading status quo.

Power-principle
Which is the dominant principle: belief or fear?
Fear.

Pay-off
What are the ulterior motives?
Neutralize the impact of game A; keep market share for yourself.

And finally, a game you can do with minimal help from me! Let's call it the mergers and acquisitions game. Let me just suggest a thesis of "shareholder value" and the pay-off of the game is to mask corporate inertia! Enjoy.

The mergers and acquisitions game

Thesis
What does the game seem to be about?
Shareholder value.

Roles
What is the role of each player?
[For you to fill out.]

Aim
What is the overall purpose of the game?
[For you to fill out.]

Power-principle
Which is the dominant principle: belief or fear?
[For you to fill out.]

Pay-off
What are the ulterior motives?
Mask corporate inertia.

APPENDIX

The Game – and What We Mean By It

An interesting approach to the "game" was set out by Eric Berne in his seminal work *Games People Play* (Penguin). Although the approach is based in psychology and psychoanalysis, the structure of what constitutes a game – and how it is differentiated from a set of manoeuvres, for example – is apposite to the tasks here.

Berne writes:

> "A game is a series of complementary ulterior transactions progressing to a well-defined, predictable outcome. Descriptively, it is a recurring set of transactions, often repetitious, superficially plausible, with a concealed motivation; or more colloquially, a series of moves with a snare, or 'gimmick'. Games are clearly differentiated from procedures, rituals and pastimes by two chief characteristics: (1) their ulterior quality and (2) the pay-off.
> "Every game ... is basically dishonest."

Points of real interest:

- The notion of "concealed motivation" – i.e. that the player has an ostensible gambit that conceals his/her real intent.

- This intent is revealed when you examine the pay-off, for that is the key to tracking back over the maneuver to discover the real but concealed intent.
- This concept of ulteriority (ulterior motive) is that which differentiates the activities from a set of operations designed to achieve an end.

Conceived thus, many daily and regular management relations with staff could be conceived of as a "game."

In many respects a good manager is one who often attempts to mobilize an employee precisely by masking the real intent.

Game example

A manager initiates a team-wide training program, providing each team member with a selection of three courses – the individual has to pick two. The stated aim is to increase and maintain customer focus and levels of satisfaction. The real intent is to get employee A, a senior member of the team who has been a continued center of team squabbles, to go on a course to deal with his poor interpersonal skills. This is clearly a ruse (admittedly elaborate) to avoid embarrassing A about his shortcomings which, in this instance, would have been deemed to be counterproductive.

Elements of the game

The game concept can be broken down into a series of elements:

Thesis \ Roles \ Aim \ Power-principle \ Pay-off

What does the game seem to be about?

This is a general description of the game – how it plays out at surface level. In the simple instance of the manager getting employee A onto a programme to deal with his interpersonal shortcomings, the thesis would be something like:

"OK team, this coming quarter I would like us all to pick two of the three programs that I am going to supply to you – as part of our ongoing drive to increase quality and customer satisfaction."

There is a choice built in – so that each individual program is not seen as enforced – yet it happened that two of the three offered to A deal with the issue of team building. He has no real choice here.

The surface-level orientation is external – i.e. getting increased satisfaction levels among the customer base – an unarguable gambit. The thesis needs to revolve around a shared value – here the value is related to training and self-betterment.

| Thesis | **Roles** | Aim | Power-principle | Pay-off |

What is the role of each player?

In Berne's terms, games are played with participants who have differentiated roles: In the example above, it is at least a "three-hander":

1 employee A – the "wrong-doer" who is at the centre of repeated complaints from the rest of the team
2 team on the receiving end of employee A's poor interpersonal skills
3 the coach: the manager who arbitrates in order to effect a more harmonious and perhaps more productive team environment, in whose name the action is proposed in the first place. In this sense the role performed by the customer is to legitimate the course of action.

Of course, from employee A's perspective, he/she might actually be the victim both of continual sniping and lack of collegiality from the team generally, and the subject of poor understanding from the manager who is wasting precious time sending the whole team on training courses when he in fact should get rid of half of them! But that is a whole different game.

Thesis **Roles** / **Aim** \ **Power-principle** \ **Pay-off**

What is the overall purpose of the game?

This is the overall purpose of the game – why this set of maneuvers has been initiated in the first place. In the example above, it is clearly desirable to get better team-based relations underway, because of a series of complaints regarding employee A's behavior.

Thesis **Roles** / **Aim** / **Power-principle** \ **Pay-off**

Which is the dominant principle: belief or fear?

For a power relationship to be established, there needs to be a connection made between the "supervisor" and the individual or group being governed. There will be a dominant principle governing the way in which this relationship actually functions – *belief* or *fear*; often a mixture of both. See the section introducing the power doughnut for a detailed exploration of how belief and fear can be produced and how they can function in establishing a power relation.

Thesis **Roles** / **Aim** / **Power-principle** / **Pay-off**

What are the ulterior motives?

This quite often is the real key to differentiating the ostensible from the real intent of the maneuver. The ostensible reason for sending the team on the training was to maintain focus on customer satisfaction. The "pay-off," presuming that the game is a success, results in modified behavior from employee A and greater and more productive activity from the team generally, i.e. the real reason all along.

Index